ANCIENT EGYPTIAN
WONDERS

The Pyramids of Giza

Charles and Linda George

ReferencePoint
Press®

San Diego, CA

© 2013 ReferencePoint Press, Inc.
Printed in the United States

For more information, contact:
ReferencePoint Press, Inc.
PO Box 27779
San Diego, CA 92198
www.ReferencePointPress.com

LIBRARY OF CONGRESS CATALOGING-IN-PUBLICATION DATA

George, Charles, 1949-
The pyramids of Giza / By Charles and Linda George.
   p. cm. -- (Ancient Egyptian wonders series)
Includes bibliographical references and index.
ISBN 978-1-60152-258-0 (hardback) -- ISBN 1-60152-258-4 (hardback)
 1. Jizah (Egypt)--Antiquities--Juvenile literature. 2. Pyramids of Giza (Egypt)--Juvenile literature.
I. George, Linda. II. Title. III. Series: Ancient Egyptian wonders series.
DT63.G45 2012
932--dc23
                                                                                    2012000282

CONTENTS

A Timeline of Ancient Egypt   4

Introduction   6
  The Search for Eternity

Chapter One   11
  Evolution of the Giza Pyramids

Chapter Two   21
  Pyramids and the Afterlife

Chapter Three   34
  Stone by Stone

Chapter Four   46
  In and Around the Pyramids

Chapter Five   59
  By the Sweat of Their Brows

Source Notes   72

For Further Research   74

Index   76

Picture Credits   80

About the Authors   80

A TIMELINE OF ANCIENT EGYPT

Editor's note: Dates for major events and periods in ancient Egyptian history vary widely. Dates used here coincide with a timeline compiled by John Baines, professor of Egyptology at University of Oxford in England.

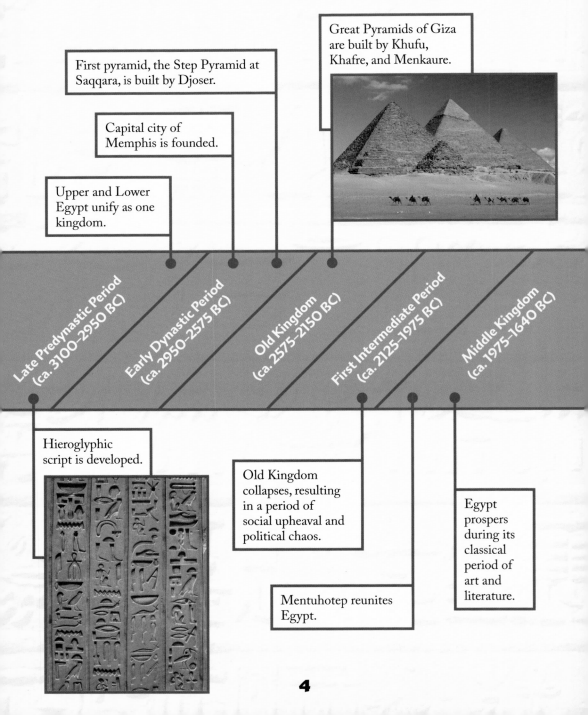

Great Pyramids of Giza are built by Khufu, Khafre, and Menkaure.

First pyramid, the Step Pyramid at Saqqara, is built by Djoser.

Capital city of Memphis is founded.

Upper and Lower Egypt unify as one kingdom.

Late Predynastic Period
(ca. 3100–2950 BC)

Early Dynastic Period
(ca. 2950–2575 BC)

Old Kingdom
(ca. 2575–2150 BC)

First Intermediate Period
(ca. 2125–1975 BC)

Middle Kingdom
(ca. 1975–1640 BC)

Hieroglyphic script is developed.

Old Kingdom collapses, resulting in a period of social upheaval and political chaos.

Egypt prospers during its classical period of art and literature.

Mentuhotep reunites Egypt.

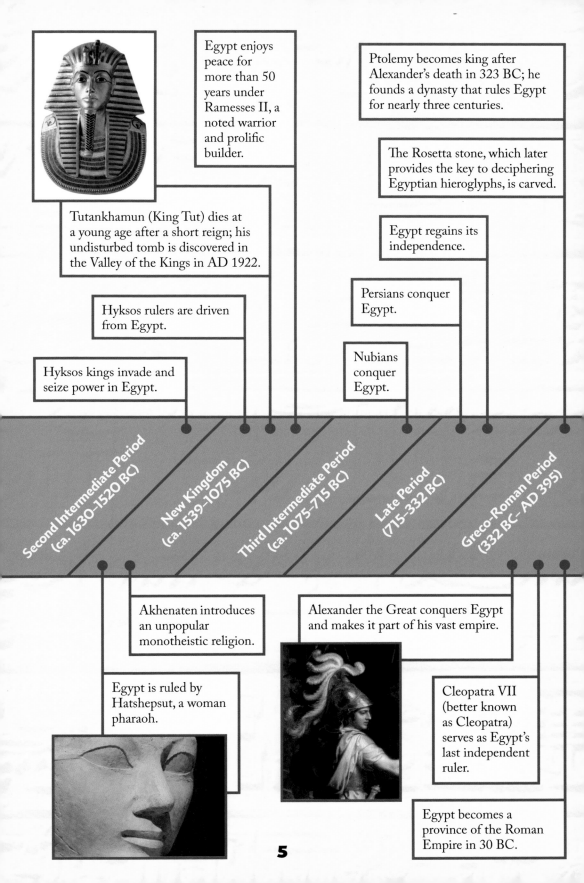

Egypt enjoys peace for more than 50 years under Ramesses II, a noted warrior and prolific builder.

Ptolemy becomes king after Alexander's death in 323 BC; he founds a dynasty that rules Egypt for nearly three centuries.

The Rosetta stone, which later provides the key to deciphering Egyptian hieroglyphs, is carved.

Tutankhamun (King Tut) dies at a young age after a short reign; his undisturbed tomb is discovered in the Valley of the Kings in AD 1922.

Egypt regains its independence.

Hyksos rulers are driven from Egypt.

Persians conquer Egypt.

Hyksos kings invade and seize power in Egypt.

Nubians conquer Egypt.

Second Intermediate Period (ca. 1630–1520 BC)

New Kingdom (ca. 1539–1075 BC)

Third Intermediate Period (ca. 1075–715 BC)

Late Period (715–332 BC)

Greco-Roman Period (332 BC– AD 395)

Akhenaten introduces an unpopular monotheistic religion.

Alexander the Great conquers Egypt and makes it part of his vast empire.

Egypt is ruled by Hatshepsut, a woman pharaoh.

Cleopatra VII (better known as Cleopatra) serves as Egypt's last independent ruler.

Egypt becomes a province of the Roman Empire in 30 BC.

INTRODUCTION

The Search for Eternity

Seventy days had passed—70 days since their king had died. All prescribed rituals had been followed by the priests, with loving care and reverence for their god-king. His body had been carefully washed, purified, and drained of all fluids. Most of his internal organs had been removed, preserved, and placed in special containers, his flesh dried with native salts and wrapped in resin-soaked linen bandages. Every requirement had been meticulously followed, adhering to religious dictates dating back to the creation of the earth by the god Atum. All this was done to ensure that their god-king would live forever. Seventy days were devoted to getting the king's body prepared. His tomb, one of the grandest the world has ever seen, took much longer to prepare. This was ancient Egypt, the king was Khufu, and his tomb was the Great Pyramid of Giza.

> **DID YOU KNOW?**
> When Jesus was born, the pyramids of Giza were already 2,500 years old.

After being mummified, Khufu's body was ready to be entombed in a huge edifice that was the most important building constructed during the king's reign—the pyramid where his preserved body would rest for all eternity. But his soul would not be trapped inside the pyramid. Thanks to carefully constructed pathways to the outside, the king's soul and spirit would fly free into paradise, where he would live forever in luxury, peace, and beauty.

WONDERS OF THE ANCIENT WORLD

Three of the grandest of all the pyramids built by the pharaohs of Egypt still stand on the Giza Plateau, just outside Cairo. These monuments to their kings—Khufu, Khafre, and Menkaure—are testaments in stone of the achievements of the ancient Egyptians. They have stood for 4,500 years as reminders of their builders and of the glory and grandeur that was ancient Egypt.

The Great Pyramid of Khufu—the first pyramid built on the Giza Plateau—became one of the Seven Wonders of the Ancient World. Today it is the only one of those structures still standing. Individuals who have visited the Giza pyramids, marveling at their existence, include Greek historian Herodotus, who visited Egypt circa 449 to 430 BC; Arab caliph Abdullah al-Mam'ūn, the first person to enter the Great Pyramid of Khufu, in AD 832; Napoleon and his invading army, who gazed upon the pyramids and the Sphinx in 1798; and American author and humorist Mark Twain in 1867. Countless others have wondered at the sight.

IMMENSE STRUCTURES BUILT BY HUMAN HANDS

Today thousands visit the Giza Plateau each year. No matter who the visitors are, when they approach the pyramids for the first time, they are awestruck at the sheer immensity of the ancient structures. The pyramids exude power and authority and engender disbelief that such monuments actually could have been built by ordinary human beings. And yet they were. Craig B. Smith, an engineer and expert in construction techniques, became fascinated by the enormity of the task of building the Giza pyramids. Smith writes:

> The majesty of the ancient Egyptians' thinking and the magnificence of their achievements are quite simply breathtaking. Could *we* have accomplished what they did without modern technology and equipment? Could *we* have done it without the pulley, the compass, or the wheel? . . . I simply *must* find out how these structures were built. . . . My mind keeps asking: how? *How?*[1]

It was once commonly believed that these incredible monuments were built by Hebrew slaves, but that theory is false. It is now known that these pyramids were built by Egyptian work crews centuries before the Hebrews were enslaved in Egypt. It is also known today that the workers who built the pyramids at Giza lived in a city near the construction site, were well fed and well cared for, and were proud to play an essential role in the preparation for their king's afterlife. After all, Egyptian pharaohs were considered living gods.

Pyramids were built as tombs for Egyptian kings—pharaohs, living manifestations of the sun god—when they departed the earth to dwell for eternity in a carefully planned afterlife. According to Zahi Hawass, Egypt's best-known and most prominent archaeologist:

> The building of the pyramids was the national project of Egypt. Every household in Upper and Lower Egypt participated in the building of the king's pyramid by sending workforces, food, and supplies. They did this to help the king be a god; the pyramid was the ladder that the king would climb to the afterlife on his quest for immortality.[2]

LADDER TO ETERNITY

Constructed between approximately 2551 and 2528 BC, the Great Pyramid stands today as testimony to the vision of its creator, Khufu, and to the skills and artistry of Hemiunu, Khufu's vizier—his highest adviser and the overseer of all the pharaoh's projects. The pyramids of Khufu's son, Khafre, and of his grandson, Menkaure, built during their reigns, stand nearby. Together they demonstrate the continued excellence of Egyptian construction techniques that had been refined and perfected since the building of the first pyramid by King Djoser, who ruled Egypt from about 2630 to 2611 BC. Exactly

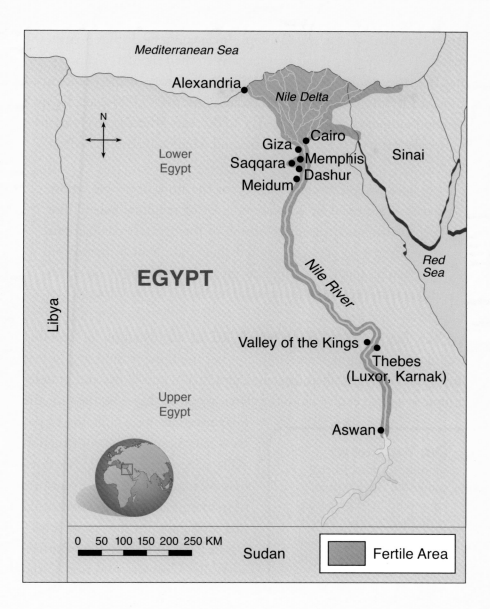

how these incredible structures were conceived and built is still being deciphered through careful excavation, examination, and study.

Archaeologists and other scientists have found clues to how their construction was accomplished, but nothing has come to light that explains definitively how thousands of gigantic stones, each weighing tons, were moved from nearby quarries, then raised and positioned with mathematical precision into the geometric figure known as a pyramid.

And yet the fact that it *was* accomplished cannot be disputed, since the pyramids themselves stand as testimony to their builders' skills.

The story of the pyramids of Giza is the story of the grandeur of ancient Egypt, a civilization that endured for over 3,000 years. Egypt's stone monuments still stand nearly 4,500 years after they were built—a virtual eternity for Khufu, Khafre, and Menkaure. Smith writes:

> Go back forty-five centuries . . . for the story of people whose lives were guided by an elaborate set of religious beliefs that formed the underpinnings of one of the greatest civilizations of all time—people who crafted their statement to history in spectacular form, creating the greatest structure[s] on earth and celebrating the human mind and spirit in the process.[3]

The Egyptians' religious beliefs led to an evolution of building techniques that grew from simple burial mounds of mud and stones into stone benches called mastabas, and finally into larger and grander monuments that evolved into the classic pyramid shape. By the time the Giza pyramids were built, the Egyptians had mastered the construction skills necessary to build the three massive monuments on the outskirts of modern Cairo—monuments that may well stand for the rest of time.

In 1980 noted broadcast journalist Walter Cronkite summed up the astonishing impact of ancient Egypt in general, and of the pyramids of Giza in particular, on history. He also tried to put the extraordinary age of the pyramids into perspective: "When Moses was alive, these pyramids were a thousand years old. Here began the history of architecture. Here people learned to measure time by a calendar, to plot the stars by astronomy and chart the earth by geometry. And here they developed that most awesome of all ideas—the idea of eternity."[4]

DID YOU KNOW?

In biblical times, Joseph convinced the Egyptian king to fill huge granaries with grain because he felt Egypt should have enough food stored to feed Egypt during seven years of famine. Some believed that the pyramids of Giza were Joseph's granaries.

CHAPTER 1

Evolution of the Giza Pyramids

The design and construction methods used to build the Great Pyramid of Khufu did not spring fully formed from the imagination of a single architect. Instead, the builder of this magnificent structure learned from builders who came before. Aware of the failures and successes of previous pyramid builders, Hemiunu—Khufu's vizier and chief builder—knew how to construct what would become the tallest building on earth for 4,300 years. The earlier pyramids built by pharaohs of the Third Dynasty still stand at Saqqara, Meidum, and Dahshur, upriver from the Giza Plateau. How they were constructed demonstrates a clear evolution of building techniques that enabled Hemiunu to build the Great Pyramid.

MASTABAS

The three main pyramids at Giza were tombs built to house the mummified bodies of Kings Khufu, Khafre, and Menkaure. But Egyptian tombs were not always shaped like pyramids, and burial chambers were not always within the interior of pyramids, as they are at Giza. Tombs built for rulers of the First and Second Dynasties at Abydos and Saqqara featured underground burial chambers that included rooms for not only the king, but also for his faithful servants, family members, wives, pets, and court jesters. There is evidence that First Dynasty king

Djer, who ruled Egypt around 2900 BC, was buried with almost 600 members of his court, so he would have servants in the afterlife.

By the end of the First Dynasty, human sacrifices at the death of a king had ceased. Above the burial chambers of a typical early Egyptian ruler's tomb, a huge mud-brick mound was built, fashioned to simulate the mound of creation—a feature of Egyptian mythology. This mound was called a mastaba ("bench" in Arabic). The oldest mastaba dates to the reign of King Menes, founder of the capital city of Memphis during the First Dynasty, around 2920 BC. His burial chamber was divided into 27 rooms to hold funerary equipment such as wine jars and food containers. Below ground were five brick-lined compartments, each with a wooden roof. The center compartment was probably the burial chamber, while the two compartments on either side contained the earthly possessions of the deceased king.

> **DID YOU KNOW?**
> Each of the six layers of the Step Pyramid required about three years to complete.

At Saqqara, more than a dozen First Dynasty tombs have been discovered, each topped with a large mastaba. The size of these mastabas ranges from 79 to 187 feet (24m to 57m) in length and 39 to 85 feet (12m to 26m) in width. Their original height was estimated to have been about 9.8 to 16.4 feet (3m to 5m), making the smallest approximately the size of eight typical city buses, parked side by side.

THE STEP PYRAMID

Mastabas continued to be erected above underground burial chambers until the second king of the Third Dynasty came to power. He wanted to build something grander as his final resting place. His name was Djoser, and his reign lasted 19 years, from about 2630 until 2611 BC. His reign marked the beginning of the first golden age of ancient Egyptian history, which some call the age of the pyramid. Djoser ordered Imhotep, his chief architect, and primary counselor, to design and construct a massive mastaba over his underground tomb. He also ordered that a temple complex be built surrounding the tomb, making it Egypt's first royal stone complex.

The Step Pyramid at Saqqara (pictured) was built by Djoser (inset), who ruled during Egypt's Early Dynastic Period. The pyramid consists of a series of mastabas, each one smaller than the one below it.

The underground complex had a maze of corridors and rooms that stretched nearly 3.7 miles (6km) and were connected to a central vertical shaft measuring 23 feet (7m) square and 91.9 feet (28m) deep. The subterranean corridors and rooms included Djoser's burial chamber, chambers for burial of his family members, and rooms for his possessions, for use in the afterlife.

Once the first mastaba had been built, Imhotep placed a slightly smaller second mastaba on top of the first. Then followed a third, fourth, fifth, and finally a sixth, creating a massive series of steps leading toward the heavens. No one is certain whether Imhotep or Djoser came up with this idea, but the innovation would live forever in Egypt, serving as a template for incredible monuments to come.

Djoser's Step Pyramid, as it came to be called, was the world's first tomb structure of such magnitude to be built entirely of stone. The finished pyramid may have measured 397 by 358 feet (121m by 109m)

THE SED FESTIVAL

The Sed festival, also known as Heb Sed or Feast of the Tail, celebrated the inauguration and reign of a king and the continuation of that reign after death. The name came from an Egyptian wolf god named Wepwawet, or Sed. The five-day festival was usually held after a king had occupied the throne for 30 years, but if the king needed to emphasize his power and authority, it could be held after only 10 years on the throne.

After the death of the king, the festival was held for the king's statue in his burial chambers. The festival included a grand procession, followed by rituals, offerings, and the symbolic raising of a *djed*, the sacrum of a bovine spine, which was a phallic symbol to represent the potency and strength of the king's rule.

A Sed festival was held for King Djoser at the Step Pyramid for Djoser's statue, which looked through a hole in the wall of the room where it was entombed. Khafre's statue was moved into the chamber so the statue could observe the rituals being performed in Khafre's honor. Those rituals might have been part of the Sed festival.

at the base and may have reached a height of 197 feet (60m). In order to ensure stability, Imhotep designed each layer carefully, making sure the stones in the upper layers leaned slightly inward for stability. Some scholars believe outer casing stones may have been set in place, possibly converting the stepped sides to smooth sides, but then were later removed to be used in other construction. So far though, no proof exists to support that theory. No one knows for sure what the finished pyramid looked like because only the base of the dismantled pyramid remains. No description or image of the finished pyramid has yet been discovered, but based on both the type of stone found in the rubble at the base of the structure and on the angle of the remaining stones, archaeologists believe their estimated dimensions are correct.

Djoser's pyramid was the first of more than 100 pyramids to be built in Egypt, each builder using the experience of Imhotep and architects who succeeded him, incorporating new ideas that resulted in both successes and failures. The two kings who succeeded Djoser attempted to build step pyramid complexes, but they failed.

THE PYRAMID AT MEIDUM

Sneferu, the first pharaoh of the Fourth Dynasty—and the father of Khufu—ushered in the next phase of the pyramid age. Zahi Hawass describes this dynasty as

> one of the most magnificent and glorious periods of Egyptian culture. In addition to architecture, the arts of sculpture, relief, and painting reach their culmination. In the natural sciences and medicine, foundations of knowledge and practice were laid that would remain valid for centuries, right into the Greek era. The belief in the almighty sun god Re, creator of all things, dominated Egyptian religion, ethics, state, and society, which became open and receptive to those with the skills to work on great projects.[5]

The Meidum pyramid was just such a great project. Originally designed to be a step pyramid like Djoser's, it had seven steps instead of six. Before the fourth or fifth step was completed, Sneferu, dissatisfied by the structure's appearance or scale, ordered that it be expanded to eight steps. Later he ordered the step pyramid made into a smooth-sided pyramid. Since evidence of this exists, the Meidum pyramid is considered the first attempt to build a true pyramid.

The Meidum pyramid, however, was not the triumph Sneferu had hoped it would be. Today all that remains is a three-stepped tower surrounded by a mound of debris. Some archaeologists believe the pyramid suffered a catastrophic collapse. But when part of the debris was cleared away, no ropes, timbers, or bodies of workers were found to support that belief.

The most important aspect of the Meidum pyramid was an innovation that would be repeated in subsequent pyramids through decades to come. Previously, the burial chamber had been constructed underground. But in the Meidum pyramid, a long passage extended from the north face of the pyramid to a burial chamber lying at about the original ground level, meaning the burial chamber lay above ground.

Two rooms opened from the corridor, with a vertical shaft at the end of the corridor leading upward into the burial chamber. Sneferu's builders were trying to create a room within the body of the pyramid. To keep the massive weight of the stone above the room from collapsing into the chamber, a stone roof was created over the chamber. This was accomplished by positioning each level of blocks inwards above a certain height until the sides almost met. This type of roof is called a corbelled roof. The roof in this pyramid is small—only 19 feet (5.9m) long and 9 feet (2.65m) wide—and was never finished. Logs were fitted near the top of the chamber at the north end between the corbelled walls.

> **DID YOU KNOW?**
> The Bent Pyramid was roughly half the volume of Khufu's Great Pyramid.

THE BENT PYRAMID

During the construction of the Meidum pyramid, Sneferu decided to move his court to Dahshur, less than 10 miles (16km) to the south. At Dahshur he ordered the construction of a second pyramid. This one, however, met with disaster when it was only half finished. Originally

MORE THAN JUST A PYRAMID

From the time of Djoser all the way through the reigns of Khufu, Khafre, and Menkaure and beyond, the pyramid was only part of what was built to honor each god-king. Each pyramid was the center of a large pyramid complex consisting of walls and other buildings. The pyramid complexes at Giza included smaller pyramids for the king's wives; a satellite pyramid known as the tomb, where the king's *ka*, or spirit, was thought to dwell; a mortuary temple with an open courtyard and an entrance hall where priests continued the worship of their god-king after his death; and a causeway, or raised pathway, leading into the temple. Some pyramid complex structures were made of mud bricks, so they have not stood the test of time as durably as their centerpiece, the king's pyramid. But ruins of their foundations and sometimes what is left of their walls remain at Giza, along with ruins of the mud-brick enclosure wall that surrounded the complex and the pyramid itself.

intended to be much smaller, with a slope of about 60 degrees and stones angled inward for stability, the pyramid began to subside, or sink into the ground, thus jeopardizing its stability. Builders added a girdle around the pyramid's base, increasing its eventual finished size, and its slope was decreased to 55 degrees. Unfortunately, these adjustments were not enough. American Egyptologist Mark Lehner explains:

> Even at the reduced angle it appears that there were still major problems until about half way up, the builders began to set

the courses [rows of stones bound together by mortar] horizontally. It had become clear that the inward-leaning courses, far from aiding stability, actually increased the stresses on the pyramid. The Bent Pyramid was then continued at a much decreased slope of around 43 degrees to 44 degrees, giving it a pronounced bend.[6]

Like his first, Sneferu's second attempt—now called the Bent Pyramid—was not what he had envisioned. He ordered construction of a third pyramid that would avoid all the problems encountered while building the first two and that would, he hoped, achieve everything his earlier efforts had failed to achieve and provide him with a tomb worthy of a great king.

The ruler Sneferu envisioned a grander version of Djoser's Step Pyramid when he ordered construction of his own pyramid at Meidum, but little remains of the structure (pictured) today. The one striking feature of this pyramid is an aboveground burial chamber.

THE RED PYRAMID

After 30 years as Egypt's ruler, Sneferu still did not have what he considered a tomb grand enough to house his body after death. In spite of its imperfect shape, he ordered builders to finish the Bent Pyramid, but he also began construction farther north on what came to be known as the North (or Red) Pyramid of Dahshur. The reddish-pink limestone used to build this pyramid suggested its name, since that stone shines red in the sun. This pyramid was built at a gentler slope of 43.4 degrees and rose 345 feet (105m) to a perfect point, with a base length of 722 feet (220m).

Pieces of the pyramid's limestone casing stones have been found, along with pieces of the capstone—or pyramidion—which is approximately 3.3 feet (1m) square at the base. These fragments indicate that the casing stones, just as they were at Meidum and from the Bent Pyramid at Dahshur, were stripped later to be used in other construction projects.

> **DID YOU KNOW?**
> More than 40,000 stone vases containing offerings to Djoser were placed in the burial chambers beneath the Step Pyramid.

Inside the Red Pyramid is a burial chamber built much like the ones at Meidum and inside the Bent Pyramid. A long corridor descends from high on the north side of the pyramid to three chambers with corbelled roofs, much more finely built than those at Meidum. A second antechamber measures 50 feet (15m) to the apex of the truly impressive corbelled ceiling. A third chamber is located above the other two, at the end of a short tunnel. This larger third chamber sits at a right angle to the other two and is believed to have been the burial chamber. Human remains were found in this chamber, but they have not been definitively identified as Sneferu's.

LESSONS LEARNED

Having the Red Pyramid to study, Sneferu's son, Khufu, was able to finally perfect the art of pyramid design and construction, thus creating a structure that would better ensure his eternal reign in the afterlife. These lessons included the selection of a site that was geographically stable enough to withstand the immense weight of a gigantic stone structure without shifting or settling. Huge stone blocks had to be used for the base of the pyramid, while smaller stones needed to be used above, for easier movement and placement. The burial chamber could finally be built inside the pyramid instead of below ground level, with masonry courses placed horizontally to better stand the structural stresses above interior chambers and passageways.

Also learned from earlier pyramids was the value of building corbelled ceilings above the burial chamber and other rooms deep in the pyramid's interior. Corbelled ceilings helped distribute the weight pressing down on these rooms, preventing their collapse. Just as important was selecting and maintaining a manageable slope to the outer walls of the pyramid, to avoid structural catastrophes. A slope greater than 52 degrees could cause cracks in the stones and possibly the collapse of the entire structure long before it was finished. The measurements had to be mathematically precise to achieve the true pyramid shape.

Sixty years passed between the end of Djoser's reign in approximately 2611 BC and the start of Khufu's reign circa 2551 BC. It is conceivable that men who had worked on Sneferu's pyramids might have lived long enough to pass on their knowledge.

CHAPTER 2

Pyramids and the Afterlife

The pyramid shape was chosen for Old Kingdom tombs—and perfected on the Giza Plateau—because of the pyramid's presence and importance in Egyptian mythology and religion. In addition to simulating the mound they believed played such a crucial role in humanity's creation, true pyramids also symbolized other elements important to Egyptian life—mountains and the rays of the sun.

Mountains were sacred to the people of many ancient cultures, primarily because they believed the gods lived in the heavens. So the higher a temple or tomb could be built, the closer it was to the dwelling place of the gods. Pyramids served as artificial mountains, helping their builders approach their gods and providing them a stairway to the heavens. Secondly, the pyramid's shape mimicked the beneficial rays of the sun streaming to earth from the sun god. Finally, pyramids echoed the shape of an artifact revered and considered a gift from the gods—the *bn bn*, or *benben*, a stone considered by ancient Egyptians to be the perfect solar symbol.

> **DID YOU KNOW?**
> Thousands of mummies of animals, including dogs, cats, baboons, crocodiles, cattle, birds, fish, and scarab beetles, have been found in Egyptian tombs, demonstrating the importance of animals to Egyptians.

THE *BENBEN* STONE

The root word, *bn*, meant "to swell up" or "to swell forth," just as the creation mound swelled up from the primordial waters that covered the earth. According to Zahi Hawass:

> [The *benben* stone] was an icon not only of the primeval mound but also of the sun, which first rose from it; the Egyptian word for the rising of the sun is *wbn*, which comes from the same root as *benben*. From the beginning, therefore, the pyramid shape represented the notion of new life, emerging both from a mound of earth and in the light and warmth of the sunrise. . . . [The *benben*] incorporated the very power of life itself, the force that made it possible for new life to emerge after a period of dormancy.[7]

The original *benben* stone may have been a rock that was naturally rounded at the top, or possibly even a pyramid-shaped meteorite. Hawass writes:

> This artifact was kept in the main temple at On, northeast of modern Cairo, which is known to us by its Greek name of Heliopolis ("city of the sun") and was the center of solar worship in pharonic Egypt from at least the Old Kingdom on. . . . In yet another version of this tale, the *benben* arose from the vast waters. The sun god, in the shape of a phoenix (the benu bird), stood on this stone. Inscriptions from later in the Old Kingdom refer to the capstones of pyramids as "*benbenet*," a clear reference to the *benben* stone.[8]

Heliopolis, like all other cities of ancient Egypt, lay along a narrow strip of fertile land in the Nile valley. Outside that limited space, life was difficult, if not impossible. In truth, Egypt was (and is) a gift of the Nile.

OPENING OF THE MOUTH CEREMONY

After the king's mummified body was carefully carried into the pyramid to the burial chamber in a wooden casket, priests conducted a ceremony to ensure that the god-king's senses would be functional in the afterworld. The Opening of the Mouth ceremony was performed before the mummy was lowered into the sarcophagus, where it would spend eternity.

According to the *Pyramid Texts* that date to the Fifth Dynasty, either a statue of the king or his death mask was placed over the mummy's head and shoulders, anointed with unguents, or salves, and its eyes smeared with paint. Then the statue or mask was washed, and offerings were placed before it. Using a tool that had been used in the building of the pyramid—usually an adze called *pesh kef*—a priest lightly tapped the mouth of the king's likeness.

Linen covering the mouth of the mummy was also cut, and milk was dribbled onto the king's lips. This "opened" his mouth and other senses. Priests and family members stood around the coffin, repeatedly chanting, "You are pure." Animals were slaughtered and left in an adjacent chamber to provide food for the king on his journey to the afterlife.

YEARLY CYCLES OF THE NILE

Egyptian belief in an afterlife began with the River Nile. Egyptians came to depend upon the yearly flooding of the Nile, although they probably were unaware of the rains that fell far to the south, in equatorial Africa, that caused the annual flooding. According to the editors of Time-Life's *The Age of God-Kings*:

Beginning in late spring, monsoon winds sweeping from the Indian Ocean dumped torrential rains on the highlands of East Africa, feeding the tributary known as the Blue Nile. That swollen branch roiled northward through mountain gorges, tracts of marshland, and fetid jungles before merging with the White Nile near present-day Khartoum. Below the confluence lay a forbidding series of six cataracts [waterfalls]. The northernmost—or First Cataract—marked the geographic boundary of Egypt. Soon after the summer solstice, the flood surge reached the Nile Valley, a 500-mile-long cleft in the Sahara extending from the First Cataract north to the marshlands of the Nile Delta.[9]

The annual flooding of the Nile River produced the nutrient-rich farmland (pictured) that sustained the ancient Egyptians year round. The rhythms of the river also influenced their beliefs in a rich and prosperous afterlife.

The nutrient-rich floodwaters, which rose as much as 14.4 feet (4.4m) above the river's normal level, covered the farmlands Egyptians depended upon for growing crops to provide food year round for themselves, their families, and their king. And since the flood came at virtually the same time—often on the same day—every year, they believed their gods were good and benevolent and caused the flooding so Egypt would be a rich, prosperous country. After each year's flood, the water receded and planting began. At harvest, enough food was stored to feed the population until the next year's growing season.

Being able to count on these yearly gifts from the gods, and observing the yearly ritual of "life and death" of the river, led the Egyptians to feel blessed and to imagine an afterlife as rich and prosperous as the physical life they led on the banks of the Nile. Theirs was an optimistic civilization. Other civilizations that existed about the same time were not so blessed.

The Sumerians, for example, lived along the Tigris and Euphrates Rivers, in what is today Iraq. Those rivers flooded at irregular intervals, without warning, bringing famine and starvation to people who lived there. As a result, they believed their gods were heartless and cruel. Their pessimistic religious beliefs carried over into their beliefs of an afterlife, where they felt they were doomed to spend eternity in a dark cave, filled with nothing but dust and silence.

RA—THE SUN GOD

The annual cycle of death and rebirth of the Nile was echoed daily by the rising and setting of the sun. According to Egyptian mythology, the sun god—referred to as Ra (or Re)—was born each morning in the east to the goddess Nut and died each evening in the west. At sundown Ra was consumed by Nut. He then traveled through her body—the

FIT TO BE BURIED

Burial rituals for Egypt's god-kings involved between four and 16 separate steps. In some cases there were rituals within rituals. Pictorial evidence of these rituals reveal women wailing, falling to the ground in grief, tearing their clothes, and throwing dirt on their heads when the king's coffin moved past them. During Old Kingdom funerals, one woman, called the "kite," was always part of the funeral. She was either a widow of the deceased or a professional mourner. Later two kites participated, representing the gods Nephthys and Isis, who mourned the death of Osiris, lord of the underworld.

Kites are mentioned in the Sixth Dynasty's *Pyramid Texts*, along with other funeral participants. The "embalmer," called *Wet*, which means "the wrapper," was in charge of wrapping the body during mummification. The "lector priest" possessed knowledge and performed ceremonies to ensure that the king's *ka* (spirit) and *ba* (soul) would be transformed into an *akh* (the perfect form of being) in the afterlife. Without the proper rituals, Egyptians believed their god-king could not assume his rightful position in the afterlife.

underworld—and was reborn the next morning at dawn to repeat the cycle of life and death. Because the sun never failed to rise each morning, and because the Nile never failed to flood their plains with life-giving nutrients for crops, Egyptians did not fear death, and they firmly believed in a happy and glorious afterlife.

This afterlife was especially important when it came to their king—whom they considered a combination of man and god. Egyptians believed their king could enter the afterlife only if he had use of his earthly body, which had to be carefully preserved after his physical death. This was done through an elaborate ritual. The body was converted into a mummy and then entombed along with his earthly possessions, in a place where it would dwell for eternity.

If the rulers of ancient Egypt had realized that their remains and possessions could be desecrated or stolen by tomb robbers, they would have concealed their resting places without any sort of markings to identify the site. They had no such fears. They were confident that their subjects would never dare to defile their tombs. As a result, they built huge monuments to display their accomplishments so everyone could see their works and be in awe of their greatness. And these monuments were built in a shape that resembled the mound of their creation myth.

THE EGYPTIAN HEREAFTER

According to Egyptian creation mythology, the earth began in darkness. Then a huge ocean called Nu appeared. From this ocean rose a mound, and from the mound came Ra, the sun god. Ra created the earth and sky. His tears fell to earth and created the first men and women. But to the Egyptians, humans were not merely physical beings. Each individual consisted of various physical and spiritual elements. The physical body was *sah*. The heart was *ib* and thought to be the center of a person's emotions and intelligence. Egyptians believed a spiritual replica of each person was created at birth by Khnum, the creator god. This replica was the *ka*. The soul or personality of the person was the *ba*. The person's name was the *ren*, and the person's shadow was the *shuwt*.

> **DID YOU KNOW?**
> During its long history, Egypt's religion included as many as 2,000 different deities.

After death, the *ka* stayed in the tomb and was imbued with life through offerings. Usually, at least one statue of the person was placed in the tomb, so the person's *ka* could inhabit the statue. In paintings and writings, a human-headed bird that could move about represented the *ba*, or personality. The *ba* moved through the underworld, where it encountered trials to overcome. Then the *ba* returned to the body, was reunited with the *ka*, and became the perfect form of existence—the *akh*.

To ancient Egyptians, the afterlife could be enjoyed by the *akh* only if the deceased's family met three conditions. First, the deceased's body had to be preserved, so that it could still cast a shadow. Egyptians believed that entities that did not cast shadows were not necessarily real, so a disembodied spirit could not exist in the afterlife. Consequently, a preserved body or at least a statue of the body was needed.

Second, offerings had to be provided regularly by mourners to provide sustenance for the person's spirit. And third, the deceased's name had to be lifted in prayer so the loved one would be remembered. All of these religious elements were present in ancient Egyptian burials, no matter the status or wealth of the deceased—from the simplest sand-pit graves, with the body wrapped only in linen, to the grandest of all tombs, the pyramids. No matter what form the tomb took, though, the body of the deceased had to be carefully prepared for interment. Just as tombs evolved from simple structures into some of the greatest monuments on earth, so, too, did the ritual of mummification evolve—from a simple procedure into a much more complex one.

MUMMIFICATION

In the earliest burials of ancient Egypt, bodies were dried naturally, buried in the sands of the Sahara. This removed all moisture from the body, producing a natural mummy. Over time, though, drying the body after death became a religious ritual consisting of a series of steps that took more than two months to complete.

The process of making a mummy began with washing and purifying the body. Internal organs were removed through an incision in the abdomen or through bodily orifices. The heart, however, was left in the thoracic cavity, because it was believed to hold the personality and spirit of the deceased. Other organs that were removed were stored in containers called canopic jars, made of pottery, stone, or wood. The brain was the only internal organ discarded. It was removed with a hook-like instrument (similar to a long crocheting needle) that was thrust up through the nose and into the skull, where it was stirred around to tear apart and liquefy the tissue. Once that was done, liquefied brain tissue drained through the nose and was discarded. Ancient Egyptians believed the brain served no function—that it merely filled the space inside the skull—and therefore would be of no use in the afterlife.

Once the body had been washed, dried, perfumed, and emptied of its organs, the body cavity was packed with natron, a natural salt that leached moisture from the body's tissues. Covered completely with natron, the body dried for 40 days. As much as 75 percent of the body's weight was lost during this drying process. After 40 days the temporary packing was removed, and fresh natron, along with linen that had been soaked in resin, was inserted into the body cavity to restore the body's original shape. The mummy then resembled the person who had been preserved and would be recognized by his or her ancestors in the hereafter.

> **DID YOU KNOW?**
> After the brain was liquefied and drained from the skull during mummification, juniper oil and turpentine were poured through the nose and left in the skull to dissolve any remaining brain matter. The liquid was then drained back out through the nose.

The final steps in the mummification process included coating the body with cedar oil and scented resins, then wrapping the body in linen strips. Tucked among the layers of linen would be charms and amulets that possessed religious significance, and sometimes personal items that held special meaning. Finally, the body was placed in a coffin while priests read incantations, prayers, spells, and hymns designed to protect and guide the person through the underworld—on the way to paradise. According to Craig B. Smith:

> In the Egyptian concept of the afterlife, the deceased was expected to eat, drink, and live a life of pleasure in paradise, with a body not unlike the one he or she inhabited on earth. From this it is logical to see how the custom of mummification, or preserving the earthly body form, grew in importance.

A dismembered, burned, or incomplete body was unsuited to success in the afterlife. . . . It was important that the tomb, or pyramid in this case, be supplied with a means for the *ka* to go in and out and receive food and drink. . . . It was believed to have the power to leave the tomb, assume different forms . . . and enter heaven to live in a state of glory with the gods.[10]

Because of their belief that the spirit of the pharaoh required an open passageway to leave the pyramid in order to reach the afterlife, pyramids were constructed with tunnels and corridors that led outside the structure. If all exits were blocked with stone, the spirit would be trapped inside the pyramid for eternity. Similarly, if the mummy were destroyed, along with all the statues, he would not have a body in the afterlife, and his spirit could never reach paradise. This was a king's greatest fear.

Mummies and mummy cases are displayed at the British Museum. After making extensive preparations, including emptying the body of its organs, the ancient Egyptians placed the linen-wrapped body of the pharaoh in a coffin along with amulets and various personal items.

Stocking the Tomb—
Packing for the Afterlife

The possessions entombed with each king reveal a great deal about that king's reign—what people wore, what they ate, and the kinds of furniture they used. Unfortunately, despite Old Kingdom rulers' confidence in the security of their tombs, later generations of Egyptians did not always share their ancestors' awe and reverence of their kings. For that reason, most Old Kingdom tombs were broken into, and the possessions, treasures, and records stolen or destroyed.

In many cases the king's deepest fears came to pass. Their mummies, statues, and canopic jars were stolen or smashed. Among all the pyramids built in ancient Egypt, the larger and grander the pyramid, the bigger a target it became for thieves intent upon stealing the treasures buried within. As a result, the vast majority of Old Kingdom tombs discovered in Egypt are empty, having been breached and ransacked many centuries ago, leaving only hints of what they might have contained.

Fortunately, hieroglyphics—a form of picture-writing used in ancient Egypt—and the discovery of a few undisturbed tombs have provided archaeologists clues to develop a fairly complete picture of life during the Old Kingdom. Archaeologists entering the three main pyramids on the Giza Plateau for the first time, however, found little to help them. In each pyramid, they found long, narrow corridors leading to empty burial chambers.

In the Great Pyramid of Khufu, a few small, unidentified objects were found in an air shaft during a nineteenth-century expedition. In Khafre's pyramid early explorers found only an empty pit beneath an empty stone coffin, or sarcophagus, where the ruler's canopic jars would have been placed. Bones discovered in the burial chamber turned out to be those of a bull, thought to have been placed there much later as an offering.

Major discoveries were made inside and beneath smaller pyramids that stand near the three major structures. Because only the king could be buried in the main pyramid tomb, these smaller pyramids have long been thought to have been the tombs of the king's wives and have thus been called Queen's Pyramids. In a vertical shaft beneath one of the three Queen's Pyramids east of Khufu's tomb, items were discovered in the mid-1930s that might have belonged to Hetepheres, Khufu's mother. An empty alabaster sarcophagus was found, along with a small alabaster box in a small niche on the wall, sealed with string. This was the canopic chest that once contained the queen's internal organs. Also found were several pieces of furniture, pottery containers, disintegrated linen, and a disassembled canopy shaped like papyrus buds. A headrest and two sets of silver bracelets completed the discovery. In a satellite pyramid near Khafre's tomb, a statue-carrying apparatus was found in the 1930s. When reassembled, it became a sled for transporting a life-size statue.

> **DID YOU KNOW?**
> Up to 478.4 square yards (400 sq. m) of linen were used to wrap each mummy.

Some of the most magnificent discoveries associated with the three main pyramids at Giza have been the boat pits. Surrounding Khufu's Great Pyramid are several long pits containing full-sized boats that have been disassembled and stored in their own "tombs." Archaeologists speculate that the large number and size of these pits east and west of Khufu's pyramid resemble symbolic ports, with the ships buried there to transport Khufu on his journey from this world to the next.

THE CYCLE OF BIRTH, DEATH, AND REBIRTH

When the pyramids of Giza were built, all of the traditional religious beliefs were incorporated into their construction, just as previous architects had done when building earlier tombs. Mark Lehner emphasizes the importance of the pyramid to the ruler and to his subjects:

> For the king, the pyramid was the place of ascension and transformation. His independent modes of being—particularly his *ka*—stood at the head of all his living and dead subjects. This was particularly true in the Old Kingdom when only the king's

pyramid was inscribed with funerary texts. No wonder, then, that it was so important to take care of his *ka*, for in a sense it contained the life force of all his living subjects.[11]

Above all things, ancient Egyptians focused on the afterlife as being as rich and abundant as their physical lives were along the river Nile. The cycle of birth, death, and rebirth lived in their hearts and souls in the form of their religious beliefs, which over the centuries led Egyptian kings to build the monuments that have lasted for thousands of years.

CHAPTER 3

Stone by Stone

The Step Pyramid, Meidum Pyramid, Bent Pyramid, and Red Pyramid can be viewed as experimental steps in learning how to build a true pyramid. When Sneferu's son, Khufu, rose to power, his first priority was to plan and build a tomb for himself that would be larger and grander than any tomb ever built. And that is precisely what he did—via the engineering genius of his closest adviser, Hemiunu. In fact, Khufu's tomb—what the modern world calls the Great Pyramid—was built so structurally sound and to such a level of precision that it served as a model for all other pyramids that were eventually constructed on the Giza Plateau. Studying the materials, construction methods, tools, and instruments used, and the basic design of the Great Pyramid served as a primer for Khafre's and Menkaure's to follow.

> **DID YOU KNOW?**
> Each copper chisel used to quarry pyramid stones was worth as much as a month's wages for the stonecutter who used it.

Khufu knew that Hemiunu was the perfect architect for this project, but it is difficult to imagine how Hemiunu must have felt when charged with such a gargantuan task. Apprehension about doing something no other mortal had accomplished must have, at some time, given way to confidence that such an undertaking was not only possible, but that the end result would astonish even Khufu.

CHIEF ARCHITECT HEMIUNU

Hemiunu had learned from builders who came before him what worked and what failed when building large stone monuments. In order to please Khufu, Hemiunu knew that he must build a pyramid that would eclipse its predecessors and stand as proof that Khufu was truly a living god. But where should this pyramid be constructed? It must be on the west bank of the Nile, because west was the direction the sun god traveled, symbolizing the cycle of life. East symbolized birth and rebirth to the ancient Egyptians. West symbolized death and the journey to the afterlife.

Sneferu's three pyramids at Meidum and Dahshur—also west of the Nile—were the largest buildings in the known world, and the sheer number of them outshone every king who had reigned before him. But Hemiunu recognized their flaws. First, he could tell, looking at the collapsed Meidum Pyramid, that a solid foundation of rock was essential for a monument the size of the one he envisioned. Second, he could see from the Bent Pyramid that trying to slope the sides too steeply would end in disaster. Finally, he knew the Red Pyramid had achieved perfection in shape, but he realized that the lesser angle of its sides meant the pyramid was limited in height.

THE GIZA PLATEAU

Hemiunu undoubtedly traveled with his building foremen in search of the best site for his king's pyramid. Accompanying him was an overseer of the quarries to ensure the new site was close enough to quarries capable of providing millions of blocks of limestone for the structure. Another official, the overseer of transport, focused on being able to build a harbor and canals to channel the waters of the Nile to the site—for construction purposes, to supply the workers with drinking water, and to help transport materials by boat from other locations. According to American Egyptologist Bob Brier and French architect Jean-Pierre Houdin:

> A stroke of engineering genius led Hemienu and his team to select the Giza Plateau. He would not build the Pyramid *near* the limestone quarry; he would build it *in* the quarry. In the time of

Hemienu, the Giza Plateau was a vast, deserted, gleaming-white outcropping of limestone covering more than 100 acres. On the north side it dropped off precipitously to the sand below, but on the south side was a gentle slope leading to a second, even larger, outcropping of limestone more than three-quarters of a mile long and one-quarter-mile wide that could be used as a second quarry. By placing Khufu's Pyramid on the Giza Plateau, Hemienu could quarry almost all the stone he needed right on-site.[12]

The Giza pyramids were built from millions of blocks of limestone, some of which can be seen in this close-up view of the Great Pyramid. The limestone came from quarries located on the Giza Plateau.

Giza had solid bedrock for stability and more than enough limestone to supply the millions of huge blocks necessary for such a project. It was also near the west bank of the Nile, making a harbor and canal feasible for bringing white limestone from quarries at Turah, 8 to 10 miles (13km to 16km) to the southeast on the east bank of the Nile, and granite from Aswan, farther upriver. Hemiunu felt the Giza Plateau was the perfect location. Once he selected the site, preparations could begin.

PREPARING THE SITE

No one can know for sure how Hemiunu told Khufu about the pyramid he planned to build, but it is easy to imagine the king's awe and appreciation for his architect's vision. Hemiunu undoubtedly drew careful plans on papyrus or perhaps on flakes of smoothed limestone, and he probably built detailed scale models to facilitate the design and construction. Without meticulous planning, he knew Khufu might be left without a suitable tomb. Khufu was about 40 years old when his reign began, and construction of his tomb would take at least 20 years, possibly longer. Would he live long enough to see his tomb completed? The timetable left no room for catastrophes. In the distance, the Bent Pyramid could be seen from Giza—a constant reminder of what could happen without precise calculations.

> **DID YOU KNOW?**
> Dragging one of the 55-ton (50–metric ton) foundation stones used in Khufu's pyramid would equal the weight of dragging a fully loaded tractor and semitrailer rig—without its wheels—up the ramps and positioning it perfectly in the pyramid.

Before construction could begin, priests first blessed the site and sanctified it. A palace and other housing for administrators and court officials were built so the king, his family, and nobles could live near the site. To get the project under way, the base area first had to be leveled. Today satellite images, GPS readings, and laser transits would be used to determine precisely where to cut to level the plateau. In Hemiunu's time, of course, none of that was available. Nevertheless, using only simple tools and his own intellect, he was able to accomplish

Khafre's Pyramid

Khafre set out to build a pyramid equal in height and size to his father's. But Khafre cheated. He chose a site for his pyramid that was 33 feet (10m) higher than the site where Khufu's pyramid was built. He also increased the angle of the sides from his father's monument in order to achieve more height in a pyramid with roughly the same base measurements. However, even with the advantage of higher ground, Khafre's finished pyramid still lacked 10.1 feet (3.1m) of the Great Pyramid's height. And the top of the pyramid was twisted.

The top 65.6 feet (20m) contain smaller stones that are only about 20 inches (50cm) thick, and there is a noticeable twist at the top because the four corners were not well enough aligned to meet as planned in a perfect point. Additional evidence that construction did not meet the standard set by the Great Pyramid is the use of almost haphazardly constructed lower courses, with very rough, loose, irregularly shaped stones beneath the casing stones. These irregular layers of stone extend into the body of the pyramid, but would have been concealed by the casing stones. Khafre's pyramid is the only one of the three on the Giza Plateau with some of the casing stones still in place near the top of the pyramid.

this to a degree of precision that astounds modern engineers. Trenches filled with water could be used to determine level, but it was not feasible for a site as large as Giza, due to the dry desert climate and the inevitable loss of water through seepage. Instead, according to Craig B.

Smith: "It appears more likely that a series of benchmarks was set along the sides of the pyramid base and a level reference point established by sighting, using the square level. . . . This line was then extended the distance required, and the foundation platform, or first course of blocks (rather than the bedrock) was leveled accordingly."[13]

A square level is a frame in the shape of the letter A that sits on a crosspiece of wood. A plumb line—a string with a weight, or bob, at the end—hung from the apex of the A. Marks on the crosspiece indicated various angles, with a center mark indicating a 90-degree perpendicular. If, when the square level was placed on a surface, the plumb line hung directly in the center of the crosspiece, then that surface was level. However the leveling was accomplished, the entire site for Khufu's pyramid did not have to be leveled completely. A natural outcropping of limestone was located where the interior of the pyramid would eventually sit, so it was left in place.

PRECISE ORIENTATION

Once the site was leveled to Hemiunu's satisfaction, the proposed base of the pyramid was carefully measured and the perimeters marked on the bedrock to be as close to a perfect square as possible. The sides were oriented to face the cardinal directions—north, south, east, and west. Without a compass to determine directionality, Hemiunu and his assistants used the stars to align the sides. Several techniques could have been used to align the pyramid with the circumpolar stars, which the Egyptians called the imperishable ones because they neither rise nor set while circling the North Pole, about 26 degrees up in the northern sky. This was important to the tomb because, according to the Egyptian's beliefs, the king would join these special stars in the heavens after death. According to Zahi Hawass:

> In 2476 BC, the brightest of the circumpolar stars, Kochab [in the bowl of the Little Dipper] and Mizar [in the handle of the Big Dipper], circled the North Pole, and a line drawn between them would have intersected due north. To find true north, an

Egyptian surveyor would simply have had to hold up a plumb line at the right time of night, when the stars lay one above the other, and waited for them to line up exactly. By marking several points on the ground, a line could be drawn to indicate true north.[14]

There was more to the pyramid's orientation, though, than determining true north. The creation myth and belief in the sun god Ra made east and west important directions to Egyptians. Due to Hemiunu's skill, and that of the surveyors who carried out his orders, the Great Pyramid was situated on the Giza Plateau more precisely oriented to the cardinal directions than any pyramid built before. Mark Lehner has this to say about the surveyors' remarkable feat:

> Some religious or cosmic impulse beyond the purely practical may also have influenced the ancient surveyors, though we can only speculate what it was. Perhaps the diagonal pointed northeast to Heliopolis, the home of the *ben-ben*, and southwest, in the direction of the Netherworld entrance of the first royal cemetery at Abydos. It is certainly clear that at Giza, more than ever before, cardinality was a principal concern. Khufu's pyramid is laid out with its sides oriented almost exactly to true north—the greatest deviation is under 5' and the 4th-dynasty builders took pains to ensure that major parts of the pyramid complexes would align.[15]

Once the cardinal points had been established, a ceremony known as the "stretching of the cord" was held to mark the perimeters of the base on the ground. This ceremony included food, music, and dancing. An animal was butchered, and pieces of its carcass were buried at the four corners of the foundation as a sacrificial offering. Other offering vessels, tablets that bore Khufu's name, and models of the tools to be used to build the pyramid were also buried at these locations. These objects were thought to attract the blessings of the gods.

FIRST COURSE OF STONES LAID

The base of the pyramid was laid out to be 755 feet (230m) square—roughly the size of 10 football fields—an area of about 13 acres (5.3ha). The slope of the pyramid would be 51.9 degrees, producing a structure 482 feet (147m) tall—about the height of a 30-story building. The bedrock surrounding the perimeter was removed, creating an area of bedrock marking the base core. Around this core a platform of white limestone from Turah was built and carefully leveled—the foundation of the pyramid. Once the platform foundation was complete and a foundation ceremony held, work began in earnest.

A ramp was built extending to the quarry, which lay about 656 feet (200m) south of the construction site. The mud-brick, mud, and stone-rubble ramp was about 10 feet (3m) wide and rose slightly as it approached the pyramid. Using this ramp, stones cut from the quarry were hauled on rope-drawn sleds by teams of laborers and carefully positioned on the foundation.

Stones were cut from the quarry using copper chisels, simple drills, and wooden mallets. In order to ensure a secure foundation, the limestone blocks for the base had to be larger than any other blocks to be used in the pyramid. They weighed up to 55 tons (50 metric tons) each. Each stone was cut from the quarry by hand, using simple tools. First the vertical front face of the stone was smoothed and leveled. Then vertical channels were chiseled into each side, depending on the width and height required. These channels

> **DID YOU KNOW?**
> The Sphinx was built on the Giza Plateau by Khafre, who gave the mythical beast his own likeness.

continued being chiseled deeper and deeper on either side of the stone and continued until the required depth was reached.

The channels were cut wide enough for workers to squeeze into sideways, to cut the back of the stone from the quarry wall in the same manner. Next a narrow groove was chiseled all the way around the base of the block, defining a break plane—the line along which they wanted the stone to crack. Along the front edge, workers chiseled out five triangular indentations.

Into each indentation, workers placed a wedge. While those five workers held the wedges in place, five other workers pounded the wedges in unison with mallets. The idea was to provide an even force along the entire front edge to fracture the stone. They knew they had succeeded when they heard a muted cracking sound and felt a slight shudder in the stone, signaling that the stone had broken free. Using levers and ropes, the workers then hauled the stone onto wooden sleds or rollers, where the rough sides and edges were smoothed with chisels. Stones used on the outside of each face of the pyramid were carefully smoothed, while blocks for the interior of the pyramid were rougher and less carefully shaped. How workers cut the stones is known because unfinished ones that clearly show chisel marks, cut channels, break planes, and marks left by wedges still stand in the Giza quarry.

RAMPS

That stones could have been dragged with ropes and levered into position has long been theorized, but exactly how these massive stone blocks were moved from the quarry and up onto the pyramid is not known. Several theories have been suggested for how the stones rose to the top of the Great Pyramid. The longest-standing theory proposed that earthen ramps had been built from ground level to the sides of the pyramids. This would be feasible for the lower levels, but as the pyramid grew, the ramps would, by necessity, have had to be immense, stretching thousands of feet from the base. Another theory suggests the ramps rose in a square spiral, diagonally up each face of the pyramid as it grew. This theory, too, has problems at the upper levels.

Egyptologists and engineers have proposed various theories for how the ancient Egyptians moved the massive stone blocks from the quarries and then hefted them into place. The most common theories suggest construction of some sort of earthen ramps.

A relatively new theory, from someone untrained in Egyptology—a French architect named Jean-Pierre Houdin—suggests how the Egyptians might have done it. Houdin's revolutionary theory still uses external ramps to build the lower levels but suggests that spiraling ramps from there to the top were inside the pyramid, not outside.

A Startling New Theory

In 1999 Houdin became obsessed with figuring out how the Great Pyramid had been built. He did not believe the prevailing ramp theories answered all the questions he had about moving the stones into place. Houdin, an architect well acquainted with large building projects, constructed intricate computer-generated diagrams that demonstrated in remarkable detail how a mile-long spiral of internal ramps could have existed inside the Great Pyramid, along which each stone was dragged upward on wooden skids, turned at the pyramid's outer corners, and then dragged farther along the spiral, until it was put into place. Houdin created computer images of what the pyramid would

MOVING THE STONES

The Great Pyramid was built with 2.3 million individual stones. A few of the larger ones had a strange inscription carved into them: "This Side Up." Some archaeologists feel this suggests that the stones may have been rolled or tumbled somehow from the quarry to the pyramid. Since Old Kingdom Egyptians were thought not to have come up with the wheel, this inscription was puzzling.

Wooden devices called rockers by archaeologists have been found that date to approximately 1550 to 1070 BC, long after the Giza pyramids were built. These rockers, which were basically a pair of thick, wooden boards that curved on one side like the rockers on a rocking chair, were held together with bars and rope. One theory for their use suggests that, with four of them securely lashed onto the sides of a stone block, the block could then have been rolled from place to place with much less effort. This theory would require the stones to be of consistent size in order for rockers to have been usable on more than one block. The blocks in Giza's pyramids are not that uniform in size, however, so the use of rockers remains a mystery, along with the enigmatic inscription's meaning.

have looked like, year by year, as it was being built. When he compared them to detailed images of the pyramid today, all the pieces of the puzzle seemed to fall into place.

In 2000 Houdin presented his theory at a scientific conference in Paris. After his speech one member of the audience—a French geologist who had been part of a 1986 study of the Great Pyramid—told Houdin that his own team's computer had generated a satellite image of the pyramid that he had not understood until hearing Houdin's theory. The French team had conducted an experiment in microgravimetry—the measurement of minute differences in the gravitational field of structures or geological features to detect empty spaces within—and their instruments had produced a gravimetric image of the pyramid that clearly shows a square spiral within the Great Pyramid. The image matched Houdin's theory almost perfectly.

In order to confirm his theory, Houdin petitioned the Egyptian government and the Supreme Council of Antiquities for permission to do a noninvasive test on the Great Pyramid, using thermal photography to produce an image that reveals internal structure. But an archaeologist had just been granted permission to excavate at Dahshur, and the government required then secretary-general Zahi Hawass to be present at each excavation or investigation into Egyptian antiquities, to ensure complete adherence with council requirements. Since Hawass could not be present at both places at the same time—Dahshur and Giza—Houdin's request was denied.

There is no way to know how long Houdin must wait before he is granted permission to conduct his thermal imaging to prove—or disprove—his theory. In the meantime, the mystery of exactly how the stones were raised to the heights of the Great Pyramid remains. No less fascinating is the mystery surrounding the spaces within the pyramids—the secret entrances, corridors, and chambers whose secrets may never be revealed.

> **DID YOU KNOW?**
> The 1986 French team whose gravimetric image seems to prove Houdin's theory about internal ramps in the Great Pyramid originally believed that the image showed compacted areas on the exterior of the pyramid caused by external ramps.

CHAPTER 4

In and Around the Pyramids

ost visitors to the Giza Plateau are awestruck by the size and precision of the three main pyramids. They wander along the bases of the pyramids, listen to tour guides recite Egypt's history, and if lucky, are allowed to enter one of the pyramids, where they are further astounded by these engineering feats. Only one pyramid is open to the public at a time, while the others undergo maintenance and restoration. Many Giza visitors see only a tiny fraction of what is there.

When Hemiunu and his work crews—and later the viziers and crews of Khafre and Menkaure—built their stone monuments, the interiors no doubt offered every bit as much of a challenge as the exteriors. Hemiunu knew as he built Khufu's pyramid that leaving space inside the pyramid for the burial chamber and the possessions Khufu would need in the afterlife would mean creating ceilings above those spaces that were strong enough to hold the weight of thousands of stones above them. The same was true for corridors leading to those spaces and for the slim passageways that would allow Khufu's spirit to leave the pyramid to live in the afterlife. Hemiunu understood the physics of weight and what it would take to distribute that weight around the pyramid's interior spaces. The easiest thing to do, he knew, would be to locate the burial chamber in the earth beneath the pyramid, as had been done with the Step Pyramid and all the mastabas that had preceded it.

About 56 feet (17m) above the base, on the north face of the Great Pyramid, Hemiunu ordered a corridor to be built that descended to a chamber deep beneath the structure. During construction, however, this chamber and its connecting corridors were abandoned. Instead, Hemiunu decided to locate the burial chamber and adjoining rooms within the pyramid itself.

THE GRAND GALLERY

Approximately one-third of the way down the descending corridor, a second corridor was constructed that led upward, then branched off into a room that at first appeared to be Khufu's burial chamber. Later explorers discovered additional hidden corridors beyond the chamber, mistakenly naming this room the Queen's Chamber. No one knows the intended purpose of this first room, whether it was to be Khufu's final resting place or something else, but apparently, at some stage in the construction or design, plans changed to something much more impressive.

The corridor leading from the Queen's Chamber, as this room continues to be called, expands into an impressive gallery in which it is possible to stand without stooping, unlike in the pyramid's other

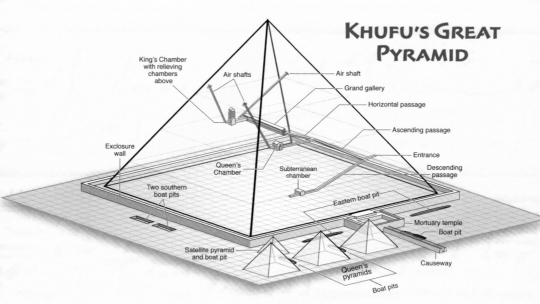

Source: Mark Lehner, *The Complete Pyramids*. New York: Thames & Hudson, 1997.

corridors. The Grand Gallery measures 28 feet (8.6m) tall, 153 feet (46.7m) long, and, at the base of the walls, 6.8 feet (2.1m) wide. This impressive corridor, apparently meant to be a prelude to the king's burial chamber, was constructed with a corbelled ceiling. The top is covered by roofing slabs that span the remaining space, measuring 3 feet (0.9m). Along the gallery are 27 niches and slots cut into the walls. Their purpose is unknown. At the end of the Grand Gallery is an antechamber, probably intended to hold personal possessions of the king. Beyond that lies the chamber for which the Great Pyramid was built.

THE KING'S CHAMBER

The room built to hold the king's sarcophagus—and his coffin within—is unlike expectations of a king's burial chamber. There are no paintings, carvings, or hieroglyphics recording Khufu's achievements. Neither is the room impressive in size. The King's Chamber is a mere 17.1 feet (5.2m) wide, 34.4 feet (10.5m) long, and 19.3 feet (5.9m) tall. Yet, in all its simplicity, it was here that archaeologists believe Khufu's coffin was interred upon his death, inside a much larger granite sarcophagus that would have been put into place as the pyramid was being built, since it is larger than any of the corridors leading to the chamber.

The King's Chamber is considered an architectural and engineering marvel. There are five additional compartments above it dubbed Relieving Chambers, because they relieve the incredible weight above them, distributing it onto the stones on either side and keeping the ceiling from collapsing into the chamber. Scholars have not seen this engineering method in any other pyramid and consider them proof of Hemiunu's architectural genius. Each

> **DID YOU KNOW?**
> To place the heavy roof beams that covered interior chambers, scientists theorize the builders may have filled the rooms with sand to create a flat surface on which to work. After the beams had been pulled into position across the tops of the walls, the sand was removed.

of the stress-relieving compartments except the top one has a flat ceiling of granite beams. The uppermost compartment has a peaked roof, to further deflect the weight from the chamber below.

Craig B. Smith, commenting on the Great Pyramid's interior, writes:

> As construction reached the level of the antechamber and King's Chamber, [the interior chambers] were undoubtedly built in place, slightly ahead of the rising terraces of the pyramid. Thus it was possible for the workmen to install the finely dressed walls, lintels, and ceiling blocks of these interior spaces from a level surface and then build the rest of the pyramid up around them as construction proceeded. This approach provided a flat working surface for maneuvering and placing the large granite roof beams and other heavy stones used in the King's Chamber and the Relieving Chambers above it.[16]

TO THE TOP

As the pyramid rose, the working surface was re-leveled an average of every 10 courses, or layers, of stone. These leveled courses correspond to the position of internal structures, such as the floor of the Queen's Chamber, the floor of the King's Chamber, and the top of the Relieving Chambers. Construction continued above the level of the stress-relieving chambers to the pinnacle of the pyramid. Once the structure had reached almost its full height, brilliant white limestone casing stones, brought on barges down the Nile from Turah, were carefully smoothed and set in place, covering each face of the pyramid from ground level to apex and creating four perfectly smooth faces.

The final step was placement of the pyramidion—a single piece of white limestone polished into the shape of the pyramid in miniature, designed to complete the structure. The pyramidion was 3 feet (0.9m) tall and had been brought to the upper levels of the unfinished pyramid once it reached about two-thirds completion. From that point, this capstone, mimicking the *benben* stone, was placed in the center of the structure and carefully raised as each stone course was added.

When the pyramid was complete, just over two decades after it was begun, Khufu must have gazed upon it with pride and an incredible feeling of accomplishment and also sadness, knowing his tomb's completion meant death was nearer. When Khufu died around 2528 BC, Hemiunu participated in his king's funeral. We can only imagine his feelings at the time. Smith speculates: "So much work, so many years, and now it was done. As he left the ceremony to return to his residence, he must have thought about Khufu. He hoped that the pharaoh's soul was at rest, that his needs for the afterlife were fully satisfied, and that now, with this structure, his spirit could ascend the stair steps to the gods."[17]

Hemiunu was afforded his own impressive mastaba tomb in the western cemetery, behind the Great Pyramid. The larger-than-life limestone statue of the architect, which the king had ordered carved and placed in the pyramid's courtyard, was moved inside Hemiunu's large, elaborately decorated tomb. After building the Great Pyramid, he had lived a happy, prosperous life, having achieved his greatest dream—and that of his king.

When completed, the Great Pyramid had 218 courses of stone from its base to its peak and stood a staggering 481 feet (146.6m) tall. At some point, the top 26.2 feet (8m) of the pyramid were removed, so today the top is a flat square, about 30 feet (9.1m) on each side. It is unknown how or why these upper stones were removed. It probably occurred when the pyramidion and outer casing stones were removed, no doubt to be used in other building projects, centuries after Khufu's reign and burial.

Near the base of the Great Pyramid, archaeologists discovered five boat-shaped pits as well as a dismantled boat most likely used only for the king's funeral procession. Archaeologists spent nearly a year reassembling the boat (pictured), which was found in more than a thousand pieces.

THE QUEEN'S PYRAMIDS AND OTHER STRUCTURES

Beside Khufu's pyramid, to the east, are three smaller pyramids. Archaeologists currently believe that the northernmost of the three housed Khufu's mother, Queen Hetepheres, and that the other two were for his wives—Queen Meretites in the center and Queen Henutsen in the southern pyramid. Some think the king's wives were entombed near him so they would accompany him in the afterlife.

The Queen's pyramids are basically step pyramids with three steps, covered with casing stones so the sides are smooth. The bases are roughly 150.9 feet (46m) per side—one-fifth the size of the Great Pyramid. The burial chambers for the queens are below ground, beneath the structures. The pyramids themselves are solid.

Also near the base of the Great Pyramid are five boat-shaped or rectangular pits. One lies alongside the causeway, two south of the pyramid, and two more on either side of the mortuary temple, built after the pyramid was completed to provide a place where priests could continue their worship of the god-king. These pits contained boats that were carefully built, used only for the ruler's funeral procession, then dismantled and stored for use in the afterlife. It took archaeologists nearly a year to reassemble one of the boats, which is 19.3 feet (5.9m) wide and 142 feet (43.3m) long. When it was found, there were 1,224 pieces, which were originally held together with rope and also with mortise and tenon joints on the hull. In this type of joint, the tenon on one piece of wood is inserted into a hole on another piece of wood called the mortise—basically inserting a tab into a slot. According to Mark Lehner:

The boats could have been symbolic transport mechanisms for the king to ascend to the heavens—westwards with the setting sun and eastwards with the rising sun—but the indications are that they fall into a different class of objects. Items connected with the royal funeral were considered in some sense highly charged. To neutralize them they were dismantled and buried separately, close to but outside the funerary precinct. ... It seems probable, therefore, that these complete, but wholly disassembled, boats were connected with Khufu's final earthly voyage—to his pyramid.[18]

SECRET SHAFTS IN THE GREAT PYRAMID

A small shaft extends from the King's Chamber deep inside Khufu's pyramid to the outside of the pyramid's face, providing a way for Khufu's spirit to leave the pyramid and enter the afterlife. The Queen's Chamber in the pyramid has similar shafts, but neither extends to the pyramid's exterior. In 1993 a robot nicknamed Wepwawet (for an ancient Egyptian god of the dead) was used to see how far the Queen's Chamber shafts extend. Wepwawet traveled only 8.7 yards (8m) up the northern shaft, until a sharp turn to the west prevented it from advancing. In the southern shaft, Wepwawet encountered a door with two copper handles 69.3 yards (63.4m) into the shaft.

In 2002 a second attempt was made to explore the southern shaft using a different robot—this one called Pyramid Rover—to drill through the door to see what lay beyond. A camera inserted through the hole, however, revealed a second door just 8.3 inches (21cm) past the first. To date, this second door has neither been opened nor drilled to see what lies beyond. The purpose of the Queen's Chamber shafts remains a mystery. They are only present in Khufu's pyramid. Neither Khafre's nor Menkaure's have such blockaded shafts.

One of the southern boat pits contained 18 cartouches—hieroglyphic carvings—bearing the name of Khufu's eldest son and heir—Djedefre—suggesting that he may have been in charge of his father's funeral.

Djedefre's Pyramid

Immediately after Khufu was laid to rest in the Great Pyramid, his heir, Djedefre, became king and moved his court 5 miles (8km) north of Giza to Abu Rawash, a hill that overlooks the Giza Plateau. There he began construction of his own pyramid tomb. Considerably smaller than his father's, Djedefre's pyramid was nonetheless spectacular, reflecting his decision to assume the title "Son of Ra." Archaeologists believe that the bottom third of his pyramid was encased in granite, with the upper two-thirds encased in white limestone.

The temple and other buildings constituting Djedefre's pyramid complex were never finished, probably because of his untimely death after only about eight years on the throne. Scholars are unsure of his fate but speculate that he was reviled at some point. They cite finding, near the ruins of Djedefre's pyramid, 120 statues of him that had been smashed and thrown into a pit. In ancient Egypt, to be remembered was to live forever. Destruction of this magnitude—the pyramid virtually obliterated and all images of Djedefre smashed—indicated that someone may have wanted to destroy him for all time—to ensure that he would not be remembered.

Some scholars believe that person might have been his half brother, Khafre, who may have exacted revenge upon Djedefre and assumed the throne upon his death. Others believe Roman invaders dismantled the pyramid after they conquered Egypt in 31 BC. A definitive answer

> **Did You Know?**
> The combined volume of the three Giza pyramids total 6.7 million cubic yards (5 million cu. m). This is enough stone to build a wall 2 feet (0.6 m.) thick and 10 feet (3m) tall that would stretch from New York City to Santa Fe, New Mexico, a distance of more than 1,700 miles (2,735.9km).

is yet to be found. The ruins of Djedefre's partially completed pyramid have only recently been discovered. Computer reconstruction, using clues from the remains of the pyramid, helped archaeologists picture the pyramid as it might have looked.

KHAFRE'S PYRAMID

When Khafre inherited the throne, he immediately began construction of his own pyramid. Like his brother, he elected to include "Son of Ra" in his title. However, he wanted his tomb near his father's pyramid, on the Giza Plateau. Using the construction techniques perfected by Hemiunu for Khufu's Great Pyramid, Khafre's pyramid is slightly

Still majestic after thousands of years, the pyramids of Giza have, in a sense, accomplished what Egypt's kings had hoped for: eternal life for them and for their civilization.

shorter than Khufu's but appears to be near the same height because the building site was 33 feet (10m) higher than the site where the Great Pyramid was built. Khafre's pyramid, completed around 2494 BC, measures 705.3 feet (215m) along each side. The slope of its sides

FANCIFUL CONSTRUCTION THEORIES

Not all theories about when and how the Giza pyramids were built can be taken seriously. One, for example, suggests that the stones for the pyramids were not quarried and dragged into place along ramps. Instead, they were poured into place—a mixture of 90 to 95 percent limestone rubble and 5 to 10 percent cement—by workers who carried the mixture in manageable buckets up the ramp to pour it into a wooden mold. Once each block dried, the molds were removed and reused. This theory, of course, ignores the overwhelming evidence that stones were cut from nearby quarries and that stonecutting tools have been found at Giza.

Another fanciful theory involves a method of levitating —floating—the stones into place. According to this theory, two pillars of unknown material became coils—one active and one passive—that generated what this theory calls a "solitron" field, or vortex, enabling priests to levitate the stones and guide them into position. The active coil supposedly tapped into Earth's "energy grid," and the "control panel" for that grid was the Hebrew Ark of the Covenant. One problem with this theory is that the Ark was not presented to humanity through Moses until more than 1,000 years *after* the Great Pyramid was built.

was increased slightly from that of his father's, to 53.7 degrees. Khafre named his pyramid "Khafre Is Great."

The interior of Khafre's tomb is simpler in design than Khufu's. According to Zahi Hawass: "The system of chambers is so simple that in the 1960s serious attempts were made by a team of prominent American scientists using the most modern technical equipment to locate additional rooms in the pyramid, without success."[19] There are admirable aspects of the interior of the pyramid, though. The large burial chamber is impressive, with a high, gabled roof. Khafre's black granite sarcophagus is imbedded in the floor of the burial chamber, but the sarcophagus and the chamber were emptied centuries before Italian explorer Giovanni Battista Belzoni found the entrance to the tomb in 1818. The top layers of the pyramid still retain the smooth, white limestone casing blocks, giving visitors a hint of the Giza pyramids' original appearance.

> **DID YOU KNOW?**
> Menkaure's dark granite sarcophagus was removed from his tomb in 1837 by British Egyptologist Howard Vyse and loaded onto a ship bound for England. The ship sank off the coast of Spain, taking the sarcophagus with it. It has never been recovered.

MENKAURE'S PYRAMID

The third main pyramid built on the Giza Plateau belonged to Khafre's son Menkaure. Compared with those of his father and grandfather, Menkaure's pyramid may seem small, but it still measured 335.3 by 343.1 feet (102.2m by 104.6m) and stood 213.3 feet (65m) tall. This pyramid, beautifully adorned with more than 16 courses of red Aswan granite around its base, might have been similar in appearance to the pyramid built by Djedefre at Abu Rawash.

Menkaure reigned peacefully for 28 years. His tomb being so much smaller than the others does not necessarily reflect Egypt's economic situation when he assumed the throne around 2490 BC, as some historians suggest. A pyramid was not only a monument to a king's power and wealth, but also a representation of the religious importance of the king who built it. Hawass describes Menkaure's pyramid: "The system of the corridors and funerary apartments in the pyramid of Menkaure is characterized by an extraordinary succession of rooms comparable only with those of Khufu's pyramid, except that those of Menkaure lead down into the rock whereas those of Khufu are ascending."[20]

Inside Menkaure's pyramid, a descending corridor enters a chamber with decoratively carved panels that are still visible. From there a horizontal corridor continues to the burial chamber, where a stunning sarcophagus fashioned from dark granite was found in 1837 by British Egyptologist Howard Vyse.

To Be Remembered Is to Live Forever

Never before in Egypt's history had such elegant and impressive tombs been built. And never again would any pyramid be built to equal those on the Giza Plateau. Khufu, Khafre, and Menkaure ordered the Giza pyramids built for several reasons. Most importantly, they wanted to be assured, through the proper rituals and preparation, that their bodies would endure for eternity. They also wanted structures that would demonstrate for eternity how powerful they were. In addition, they wanted to be surrounded for eternity with people who would continue to serve them and with possessions that would provide them the level of luxury in the afterlife they had come to expect on earth. They wisely believed that providing their subjects with a building project of this magnitude would instill pride as well as loyalty toward their king.

Khufu, Khafre, and Menkaure are remembered more than 40 centuries after they lived and died. Their names are known across Egypt and around the world. But they did not build these incredible structures with their own hands. The Egyptians who built them—those who toiled in the hot sun, stone by stone, to make them a reality—have been lost to history until recently. Now, thanks to discoveries on the Giza Plateau, these workers and details about their daily lives are slowly emerging from obscurity.

CHAPTER 5

By the Sweat of Their Brows

After more than 4,500 years, questions remain about exactly how the pyramids of Giza were constructed, but now archaeologists at least are getting to know who actually built them—and it was not aliens or alien-inspired people from the lost continent of Atlantis, as two of the more outlandish theories have suggested. During the past 20 years, archaeological evidence has been found on the Giza Plateau that these incredible monuments were, indeed, built by Egyptian artisans and laborers.

LOOKING FOR THE LOST CITY

For decades excavations on the Giza Plateau turned up only bits and pieces to suggest that the pyramid builders actually lived near the construction site. In August 1990 Zahi Hawass discovered an ancient cemetery where some of the builders had been buried. It was less than a half mile (0.8km) south of the pyramids, and so far, 600 graves of skilled workers and another 82 underground tombs containing the remains of artisans and overseers have been unearthed. The skeletal remains found in the tombs, and the personal possessions buried alongside, are providing clues about these people and the lives they lived. But where were their homes, their workshops, their warehouses?

When he learned of Hawass's discovery, Mark Lehner wondered if the homes of those buried in the cemetery might be nearby. Why would they be buried on the Giza Plateau if they lived elsewhere? He returned to Giza in 1995, determined to find where the workers had lived. Over the next four years, Lehner made a series of discoveries, what he called "small windows opening onto an increasingly intriguing settlement."[21]

In 1999 his "small windows" expanded into a huge vista when Lehner launched a massive excavation to find the homes of the builders. He describes his project: "Thus began a two-year marathon season from fall 1999 to summer 2000. We cleared and staked 413 squares—one hectare, or the area of more than two football fields. And the dramatic discoveries began."[22] Hints of bakeries, workers' houses, and workshops that had surfaced during the early phase were confirmed to be elements of a royal complex that had, as its center, the residence of the king and his royal court. The ruins of two galleries—long, relatively narrow rooms—were unearthed, separated by one of the oldest known paved streets ever found. This 17-foot-wide (5.2m) thoroughfare has been dubbed Main Street by excavators. The galleries were found to contain sleeping places for up to 2,000 workers. If there were two levels, as many as 4,000 could have slept in this barracks-like building.

As these excavations continued, the foundations of more and more buildings were uncovered and their functions identified. There were bakeries, copper works, dining halls, additional galleries, pigment grinding shops, granaries and other storage facilities, and a manor house and gatehouse. Clearly, the workers were carefully monitored, for efficiency and safety. According to Hawass:

> Every man, woman, and child was accounted for, and each item of food and clothing was recorded. We even know . . . that the workers' tools were carefully tracked. At Giza, an administrative center (a pillared building near the paved road) would have

been the central distribution point for the food consumed by the workmen. It is likely that the storage place for the tools, checked in and out by the individual workers each day, was located near this building.[23]

WORK CREWS AND HOW THEY LIVED

About 20,000 men are thought to have participated in the construction of the Great Pyramid. Graffiti left on the pyramid's stones by some of these workers, along with the hierarchical titles of other

A fragment of a tomb wall painting depicts cattle being registered and inspected. Egyptologists estimate that dozens of cattle, sheep, and goats were slaughtered every day to feed the thousands of workers needed to build the Giza pyramids.

workers, have provided archaeologists an idea about the organization of the workers into crews. At the head of all workers was the vizier, whose title was "overseer of all the king's work." Below him were several lesser overseers, who each controlled supervisors. Each supervisor was in charge of groups of workmen called crews. Each crew of 2,000 men was further subdivided into two gangs of 1,000 each. These gangs gave themselves nicknames—some serious and some not so serious. Excavators have, for example, unearthed cartouches with names such as Friends of Khufu, or Menkaure Is Drunk.

Each gang was further subdivided into four groups of 200 called *phyles*. *Phyle* is a Greek word for "tribe." *Phyles* also had names, such as Green/Prow Ones, Great/Starboard Ones, or Asiatic/Port Ones. Smaller groups of 20 to 50 workers within the *phyles* had names like Life, Perfection, or Endurance. These groups of workers apparently competed with each other to see which could cut more stones, move more stones, or place more stones each day, perhaps to earn bragging rights but also possibly to earn rewards of some type.

> **DID YOU KNOW?**
> Ruins of the structure that archaeologists believe may have been the royal palace in the City of the Pyramid Builders were oriented north and south, like the pyramids and other royal palaces.

It is estimated that the 20,000 builders lived around the king's palace in a complex of streets, houses, and common areas. It is also estimated that 11 head of cattle and 33 sheep and goats had to be slaughtered every day to feed 10,000 workmen. A text dated during Khafre's reign stated that he owned 1,055 cattle, 974 goats, and 2,235 sheep. But all the animals slaughtered during the 80 years encompassing the reigns of Khufu, Khafre, and Menkaure could not have been raised on the Giza Plateau. They must have come from people living elsewhere in Egypt who either sold or donated animals to feed the work gangs.

Scientists reached the estimate of how much meat must have been supplied to workers by the large number of fish, cattle, sheep, and goat bones that have been unearthed across the city's ruins. Appar-

LEISURE ACTIVITIES FOR THE PYRAMID BUILDERS

When Egypt's pyramid builders were not busy building, they enjoyed recreation, food, and fun, just as all people do when their day's work is done. Egyptians were wonderful storytellers, and they often entertained each other by telling tall tales about kings and commoners alike. Several of their tales have been preserved in hieroglyphics. One tells about a shipwrecked sailor who becomes marooned on an island where a huge serpent lives. Another relates the story of a prince, searching for a way to escape death, who meets a princess imprisoned in a tall tower. To escape her captivity, the princess lets down her hair, much like Rapunzel in the familiar Grimm brothers' fairy tale.

Other activities enjoyed by the ancient Egyptians included hunting, fishing, making music, and getting together for big parties, with lots of food, beer and wine, music, and dancing. Egyptians also enjoyed playing board games during leisure times. The playing boards from three of their games—Senet, Hounds and Jackals, and Mehen— have survived, but the rules for these games have not.

ently, workers on this project ate meat virtually every day, to give them strength to keep working for nine days out of every 10. Only male livestock was killed for food. Females were kept to bear offspring. Evidence of onions and garlic has been found, as well as bread and large quantities of beer that must have been brewed in the city.

Copper tools to be used by stonecutters were made or repaired in the city's workshops. Artisans of the workforce, including painters and sculptors, lived in a separate village east of the cemetery. Hawass has this to say about the artisans: "The village of the artisans at Giza shows that each artisan, draftsman, craftsman, and sculptor lived in a house consisting of a room to store his materials and a court for his work in the daylight; attached to this area would be rooms for sleeping, reception areas, for meeting people, kitchens for the preparation of food, and storage areas."[24]

REAL PEOPLE

Knowing what type of buildings were located in the city, what kind of tools the workers used, that they ate together in large dining rooms, and that they slept in barracks helped bring these people to life again. But those discoveries alone did not reveal the individuals themselves—the pyramid builders and their families—as distinct men, women, and children. Fortunately for scholars, the names of some of these ordinary people were recorded among the tombs of the pyramid builders in the Giza cemetery, finally allowing these people to be remembered as individuals.

It was written, for example, that a man named Senmeru oversaw the transportation of white limestone blocks from Turah and pink granite slabs from Aswan that were used for the casing stones. Another overseer, Merer, made sure his *phyle* made it safely to and from the construction site, that his workers were well fed, and that they drank enough liquid to stay hydrated. Wenemniut, another Egyptian worker at Giza, took care of offerings from the royal farms—grain, wheat, and cattle. Nyankhptah, a chief baker, kept watch over grain from the granaries being hauled to the bakeries so it could be baked into thousands of loaves of bread. A man named Wahy made sure the workmen's clothing was laundered and that they had clean clothes to wear each day.

DID YOU KNOW?
Ancient Egyptian homes contained rooms for bathing, and also bathrooms with toilets—a horseshoe-shaped wooden seat over a bowl of sand.

Laborers working on the pyramids required bread and beer, two staples of the ancient Egyptian diet. A model from an early period of ancient Egypt depicts kitchen workers grinding grain, baking bread, and brewing beer.

A limestone mastaba marks the graves of Nefertheith and his wives, Hyankhhathor and Neferhetepes. Nefertheith had seven children with Hyankhhathor and 11 children with Hefertheith, who was referred to as a midwife, a woman who assists other women during childbirth. In images of this family, drawn inside their tomb, Hefertheith is drawn at the same scale as her husband, indicating equal rank with him.

Illustrations inside one tomb showed the making of bread and beer. In the images, an unnamed woman strains mash through a sieve, while a man pours beer into containers. Nearby, a woman named Khenut grinds grain, while a man named Kakai-ankh tends the fire beneath bell-shaped molds of bread dough. He shades his face from the heat with one hand. These details help bring these individuals to life, 4,500 years after they lived and died. The details are making it abundantly clear that the pyramids were built by real people, with real lives and real identities.

Sometimes the unearthed images leave questions unanswered. In another burial site, for example, Pettety and his wife Nesy-Sokar are depicted, but they never appear together in the scenes. Nesy-Sokar was apparently a priestess of the goddess Hathor, and according to Hawass, "beloved of the goddess Neith [mother of Ra]."[25] On one wall of their tomb, excavators found a scene depicting Nesy-Sokar and her daughter, who is holding a bag and a mirror. The priestess, wearing a tight, wide collar, stands in the doorway of a chapel with one arm raised to her breasts and one arm behind her, with her head tilted back. Her eyes, outlined with a popular cosmetic called kohl, add confidence to her expression. Beside her image, a curse is inscribed:

> O anyone who enters this tomb,
> Who will make evil against this tomb:
> May the crocodile be against him on water,
> And the snake against him on land.
> May the hippopotamus be against him on water,
> The scorpion against him on land.[26]

WOMEN IN ANCIENT EGYPT

Unlike other ancient cultures, Egyptian women were not considered possessions of their husbands, having few rights. According to author Barbara Watterson:

In ancient Egyptian society a woman was accorded legal rights equal to those of a man from the same social class and had the same expectation of a life after death. Such consideration toward women was rare in other ancient societies. Pharaonic Egypt was not an exclusively male-dominated society in which women were regarded by men merely as breeding machines or beasts of burden. Instead, it was one in which they were allowed to exert a degree of freedom and, in some cases, influence, beyond the confines of the home.[27]

THE LOST CITY GALLERIES

One of the most exciting finds from the huge excavation conducted by Mark Lehner of the Lost City of the Pyramid Builders was the discovery of the ruins of three or four sets of huge galleries—long, narrow rooms. Each set contains eight galleries that range in width from 14.7 to 15.7 feet (4.5 to 4.8m). Each is unique, but they share similar features. Each has a complex of rooms at the southern end and an open area to the north. Low walls extend down the center of the north ends of the galleries, with stones beneath the walls, suggesting there might have been wooden columns about 9 inches (23cm) in diameter forming a colonnade of sorts to support the roof. These colonnades are some of the oldest found so far in Egypt.

Inside the galleries, walls separated rooms that could have been inhabited by workers. In some places there are areas with a small vestibule, or entryway; a main room; and smaller rooms, possibly used for sleeping. In some rooms ashes have been found, suggesting the rooms might have been used for baking bread. Recent excavations have revealed bed platforms, confirming that these structures were dormitories.

Despite this freedom, Egyptian women were expected to marry, have children, take care of the household, and defer to their husbands in many ways. Yet women were allowed to engage in professions, including being priestesses, which accorded them the highest status.

Women were usually buried with their husbands, but not always. Sometimes women were buried in separate tombs. The remains of a woman named Repyt-Hathor were discovered in her own tomb, most likely because she served as a priestess of Hathor. Another, Nugj, a priestess of the goddess Neith, was buried in a much grander tomb, indicating higher rank. Priestesses enjoyed the highest social rank a woman could achieve, but their influence was confined to the temple and religious duties and did not extend into regular society outside the realm of religion.

A major female figure from the creation myth undoubtedly set the standard for priestesses. In the myth King Osiris was killed by his brother, Seth, to gain the throne. Seth chopped Osiris's body into 14 pieces and scattered them. But Isis, their sister, was able to retrieve 13 of the pieces. The fourteenth piece—his penis—was eaten by a fish. So Isis replaced the missing piece with a golden phallus and conceived a child with Osiris. Isis provided a strong female role model for women. She became the most popular goddess in Egypt because she conquered death and resurrected her brother to an afterlife as god of the underworld, establishing the Egyptian belief in an afterlife for all people.

DID YOU KNOW?
On either side of the Lost City galleries were the Eastern Town, which was a typical village where workers and their families lived, and the Western Town, where high administrators such as the royal scribe and the overseer of the king's work lived.

Women were dominant in the textile industry, as supervisors as well as workers, weaving cloth used in clothing. They also played musical instruments or sang, and sometimes became professional mourners—wailing and weeping at funerals for money. Women also became nurses or midwives, ministering to the sick and aiding with childbirth, which at the time was one of the primary causes of death for women.

The goddess Isis, right, leads one of Egypt's New Kingdom queens by the hand in this modern copy of an original tomb painting. The popular goddess provided a strong role model for the women of ancient Egypt.

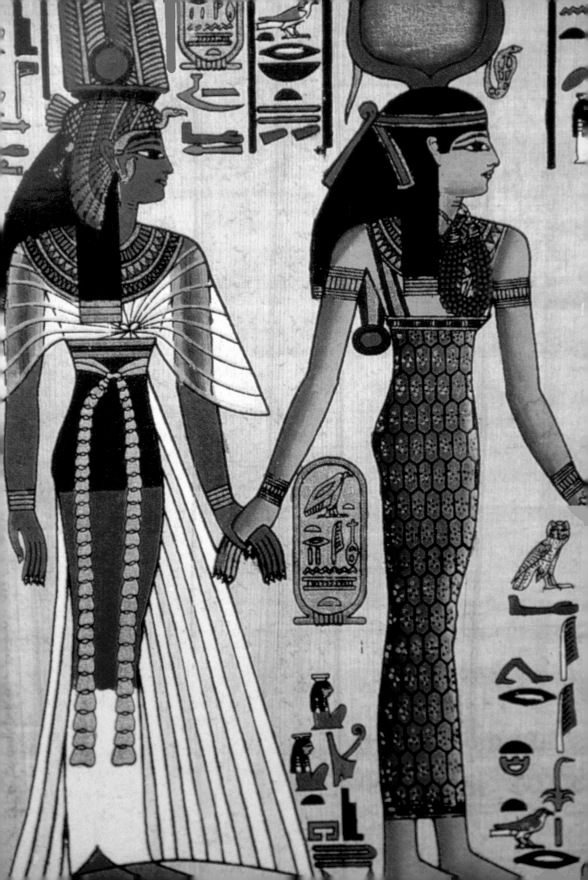

DAILY LIVES

It is evident that the pyramid builders of Giza received adequate medical attention, since skeletal remains show signs of broken bones that had been set, then healed satisfactorily. Amputations were performed, with the amputee living for years afterward. Degenerative diseases, primarily of the knees and other joints, were common among laborers, but less frequent among upper-class Egyptian citizens. Compression of vertebrae in the skeletal remains of workers has been seen, owing to decades of heavy labor which undoubtedly caused back pain. Deterioration of knees, ankles, and hips from dealing with heavy loads was also evident among the workmen. Skull and other bone fractures occurred. Surgery was often warranted, and there is even evidence of brain surgery being performed.

> **DID YOU KNOW?**
> Tourism has led to deterioration of the interior of the pyramids, caused by water vapor in the breath of millions of visitors.
> The humidity inside the Great Pyramid reaches 85 percent, thanks to each visitor exhaling about 0.7 ounces (20g) of water.

The pyramid builders and their families began their days before sunrise. It is possible that a drummer awakened them, signaling the beginning of a new day. Work continued until sunset—a 10-hour work day. The men wore a type of kilt and sandals to work. There were numerous feast days—somewhere in the neighborhood of 100 each year—but workers did not celebrate all of them. These special occasions included the feast of Djehuty (feast of the half moon), the feast of the full moon, the feast of the harvest, and the feast of Ra.

REMEMBERING ANCIENT EGYPT

What has been learned about the thousands of laborers who built the pyramids of Giza is, above all, that they were Egyptian and that they were proud to help prepare their king's tomb, ensuring him an afterlife fit for a god. It is true that Egyptians built the pyramids, but in a way the pyramids also built Egypt—into a prosperous, relatively stable country. The tombs constructed for Khufu, Khafre, and Menkaure have stood for thousands of years as monuments to these god-kings. Now that individual Egyptian workers and their families are emerging from centuries of obscurity, the pyramids of Giza are today becoming their monuments, too.

Well over 150 generations have passed since Khufu, Khafre, and Menkaure walked the earth. Countless more will pass before the stone monuments built in their honor cease to exist. Who knows? The pyramids of Giza could even outlive humanity itself, should some global catastrophe strike that wipes out life on this planet. An ancient Egyptian proverb probably says it best: All things dread Time, but Time dreads the pyramids.

SOURCE NOTES

INTRODUCTION: THE SEARCH FOR ETERNITY

1. Craig B. Smith, *How the Great Pyramid Was Built*. New York: Harper Perennial, 2004, p. 20.
2. Quoted in Smith, *How the Great Pyramid Was Built*, p. 8.
3. Smith, *How the Great Pyramid Was Built*, p. 27.
4. Walter Cronkite, *Sadat's Eternal Egypt*. Columbia Broadcasting Service News Documentary, 1980.

CHAPTER ONE: EVOLUTION OF THE GIZA PYRAMIDS

5. Zahi Hawass, ed., *Pyramids: Treasures, Mysteries, and New Discoveries in Egypt*. Vercelli, Italy: White Star, 2011, p. 128.
6. Mark Lehner, *The Complete Pyramids: Solving the Ancient Mysteries*. London: Thames & Hudson, 1997, p. 102.

CHAPTER TWO: PYRAMIDS AND THE AFTERLIFE

7. Hawass, *Pyramids*, p. 36.
8. Zahi Hawass, *Mountains of the Pharaohs*. New York: Doubleday, 2006, pp. 34–35.
9. Editors of Time-Life Books, *The Age of God-Kings*. Alexandria, VA: Time-Life, 1987, p. 55.
10. Smith, *How the Great Pyramid Was Built*, pp. 42–43.
11. Lehner, *The Complete Pyramids*, p. 24.

CHAPTER THREE: STONE BY STONE

12. Bob Brier and Jean-Pierre Houdin, *The Secret of the Great Pyramid: How One Man's Obsession Led to the Solution of Ancient Egypt's Greatest Mysteries*. New York: Harper Perennial, 2008, pp. 58–59.
13. Smith, *How the Great Pyramid Was Built*, p. 100.
14. Hawass, *Mountains of the Pharaohs*, pp. 58–59.
15. Lehner, *The Complete Pyramids*, p. 106.

CHAPTER FOUR: IN AND AROUND THE PYRAMIDS

16. Smith, *How the Great Pyramid Was Built*, p. 100.
17. Smith, *How the Great Pyramid Was Built*, p. 238.
18. Lehner, *The Complete Pyramids*, p. 119.
19. Hawass, *Pyramids*, p. 146.
20. Hawass, *Pyramids*, p. 150.

CHAPTER FIVE: BY THE SWEAT OF THEIR BROWS

21. Mark Lehner, "Lost City of the Pyramids," *Egypt Revealed*, Fall 2000, p. 47.
22. Lehner, "Lost City of the Pyramids," p. 48.
23. Hawass, *Mountains of the Pharaohs*, p. 166.
24. Hawass, *Mountains of the Pharaohs*, p. 166.
25. Hawass, *Mountains of the Pharaohs*, p. 170.
26. Quoted in Hawass, *Mountains of the Pharaohs*, pp. 170–71.
27. Barbara Watterson, *Women in Ancient Egypt*. Great Britain: Wrens Park, 1991, p. 1.

FOR FURTHER RESEARCH

Books

Bob Brier and Jean-Pierre Houdin, *The Secret of the Great Pyramid: How One Man's Obsession Led to the Solution of Ancient Egypt's Greatest Mystery*. New York: Smithsonian, 2008.

Zahi Hawass, *Mountains of the Pharaohs: The Untold Story of the Pyramid Builders*. New York: Doubleday, 2006.

Zahi Hawass, ed., *Pyramids: Treasures, Mysteries, and New Discoveries in Egypt*. Vercelli, Italy: WS Whitestar, 2011.

Mark Lehner, *The Complete Pyramids: Solving the Ancient Mysteries*. London: Thames & Hudson, 2008.

Craig B. Smith, *How the Great Pyramid Was Built*. New York: Harper Perennial, 2006.

Barbara Watterson, *Women in Ancient Egypt*. Stroud, UK: Amberley, 2012.

Websites

Egypt: Secrets of an Ancient World, National Geographic (www.nationalgeographic.com/pyramids/pyramids.html). This interactive website provides information about eight Egyptian pyramids, including the Step Pyramid of Djoser, the three pyramids built by Sneferu, and the three pyramids built on the Giza Plateau by Khufu, Khafre, and Menkaure.

Excavating the Lost City, *NOVA* (www.pbs.org/wgbh/nova/ancient/lehner-giza.html). This interview with Mark Lehner was conducted in 2009 and includes new information about the excavations of the Lost City of the Pyramid Builders on the Giza Plateau.

Khufu Reborn (www.3ds.com/company/passion-for-innovation/the -projects/khufu-reborn/khufu-reborn). This remarkable website, produced by Dessault Systemes, illustrates Jean-Pierre Houdin's radical new theory about how the Great Pyramid may have been constructed. Incredible three-dimensional animation, music, and interactivity bring Houdin's theory to life. Download required.

The Lost City, Ancient Egypt Research Associates (www.aeraweb .org/projects/lost-city). An interactive map of the Lost City of the Pyramid Builders recently unearthed near the Giza pyramids.

NOVA **Online** (www.pbs.org/wgbh/nova/pyramid/explore). Information about every aspect of the pyramids of Giza, including interactive tours of the Giza Plateau; the pyramids of Khufu, Khafre, and Menkaure; and inside the Great Pyramid of Khufu.

Ramjee's Learning: The Great Pyramid Mystery (http://ramjeen agarajan.blogspot.com/2008/11/great-pyramid-mystery.html). This site contains a video that demonstrates Jean-Pierre Houdin's theory of how an interior ramp within the Great Pyramid could have been used to build the pyramid. Also on this site is an article describing the theory and how evidence to prove it could be obtained using noninvasive tests that have already been done, with photographic evidence of Houdin's ramp.

TELEVISION PROGRAMS/DVDs

Ancient Egypt Unearthed. Discovery Channel, 2009.

History Classics: Egypt—Pyramids and Mummies. A&E Home Video, 2010.

Tombs of the Gods: The Great Pyramids of Giza. A&E Home Video, 2006.

INDEX

Note: Boldface page numbers indicate illustrations.

Abydos mastabas, 11–12
afterlife
  burial practices necessary to enjoy, 23, 28, 29–32
  circumpolar stars in, 39–40
  ka and *ba* during, 26, 27–28
  rituals for kings, 14, 23, 26–27
  symbols of, 35
Age of God-Kings, The, 23–24
age of pyramids, 6, 7
akh (perfect form of being), 26, 28
al-Mam'ūn,Abdullah, 7
animals, 21, 23, 62
Atum (god), 6

ba (soul), 26, 27–28
Belzoni, Giovanni Battista, 57
benben (bn bn) stone, 21–22, 50
Bent Pyramid, 15–19, 35
Blue Nile River, 24
board games, 63
boat pits and boats, 32, **47**, **51**, 52–54
brain, 28–29
Brier, Bob, 35–36
burial practices
  to ensure enjoyment of afterlife, 23, 28, 29–32
  First and Second Dynasties, 11–12
  location in pyramids of burial chambers, 16, 19
  neutralization of items used, 52–53
  Opening of the Mouth ceremony, 23
  professions involved, 26
  Sed festival, 14
  Third Dynasty, 12
  for women, 67–68
  for workers and families, 65
  See also Great Pyramid of Khufu

canopic jars/chests, 28, 31, 32
cardinality, principle of, 39, 40
cartouches (hieroglyphic carvings), 54, 62
cenotaphs, 15
chisels, 34, 41, 42
circumpolar stars in afterlife, 39–40
City of the Pyramid Builders, 60, 62, 67, 68
construction workers, 8, **65**
  cemetery for, 59
  daily lives of, 70
  food for, **61**, 62–63, **65**
  health of, 70
  Hebrew slaves as, 8
  homes of, 60, 64, 67
  leisure activities enjoyed by, 63
  monitoring of, 60–61
  names and jobs of, 63–64, 65–66
  number of, 61
  organization into crews of, 61–62
  village for, 60, 64
corbelled roofs, 16, 20
creation
  gods of, 6, 15, 27
  mastabas as symbols of, 12
  myth about, 27, 68
  pyramid shape and, 21
Cronkite, Walter, 10

Dahshur, pyramid at (Bent Pyramid), 15–19, 35
deities
  kings as, 8, 26–27
  See also specific deities
Djedefre (king), 54–55
Djer (king), 11–12
Djoser (king)
  Step Pyramid and, 12–15, **13**, 19
  time of rule, 8, 20

Eastern Town, 68
Egypt
  map of, 9

Feast of the Tail, 14
First Dynasty burial practices, 11–12
Fourth Dynasty. *See* Khufu (king);
  Sneferu (king)

Giza Plateau, 7, 35–37
gods
  kings as, 8, 26–27
  See also specific gods
granaries, pyramids as, 10
Grand Gallery (Great Pyramid), 47–48
gravimetric images, 45
Great Pyramid of Khufu
  age of, 8
  boat pits and boats, 32, **47**, **51**, 52–54
  burial chamber, 46–47
  construction of
    ceremonies, 40, 41
    duration of, 37, 50
    materials, 36–37, **36**, 41–42, 44, 50
    methods, 48, 49–50
    orientation and, 39–40
    site preparation for, 37–39
    theories about, 42–45, **43**, 48, 56
    tools used, 34, 39, 41, 44
  effect of tourism on, 70
  interior space of, 46–49, **47**, 50, 53
  location, 35–37
  as model for other pyramids, 34, 38
  nearby pyramids, 52–53
  nineteenth-century findings, 31
  removal of stones from, 50
  secret shafts, 53
  as a Wonder of the Ancient World, 7

Hawass, Zahi
  on artisans, 64
  on *benben* stone, 22
  discovery of cemetery for
    construction workers, 59
  on Fourth Dynasty, 15
  Houdin's theory and, 45

on interior of Khafre's pyrmaid, 57
on interior of Menkaure's pyramid,
  58
on monitoring of construction
  workers and families, 60–61
on orientation of Great Pyramid,
  39–40
on pyramids as national building
  projects, 8
health, 70
heart, 27, 28
Hebrew slaves, 8
Heb Sed, 14
Heliopolis, 22
Hemiunu, 8, 11, 34–35, 37, 39, 46–47,
  48, 50
  See also Great Pyramid of Khufu
Henutsen (wife of Khufu), 52
Herodotus, 7
Hetepheres (mother of Khufu), 32, 52
hieroglyphics, 31, 54, 63
Houdin, Jean-Pierre, 35–36, 43–45
human body, physical and spiritual
  parts of, 27–28

ib (heart), 27, 28
Imhotep, 12, 13–14
Isis (goddess), 26, 68, **69**

Joseph (biblical figure), 10

ka (spirit), 17, 26, 27–28, 30, 32–33
Khafre (king)
  expedition findings, 31
  pyramid of, 8, 38, 50, 55–57
  rituals for, 14
  Sphinx and, 41
Khnum (god), 27
Khufu (king)
  death of, 6, 50
  funeral of, 54
  pyramid design perfected under,
    19–20
  pyramids of mother and wives, 52
  time of rule, 8, 20
  See also Great Pyramid of Khufu

King's Chamber (Great Pyramid), **47**, 48–49, 53

kites, 26

lector priests, 26

Lehner, Mark
  on Bent Pyramid, 17–18
  on boats in pyramids, 52–53
  discovery of city for construction
    workers by, 60, 67
  on importance of pyramids, 32–33
  on orientation of Great Pyramid,
    40

levitation, 56

limestone, 19, 35–37, **36**, 39, 41, 49, 50, 54, 56, 57, 64, 65

Lost City of the Pyramid Builders, 67, 68

mastabas
  described, 10
  development into pyramids, 13, 13
  history of, 11–12
  as symbols of creation, 12
  of workers and families, 65–66

Meidum, pyramid at, 15–16, **18**, 35

Menes (king), 12

Menkaure (king), 8, 42, 57–58

Meretites (wife of Khufu), 52

microgravimetry, 45

mountains, sacredness of, 21

mud bricks, 17

mummification, **30**
  of animals, 21
  process of, 6, 28–29, 32
  professions involved in, 26
  reason for, 28, 29–30

Napoleon, 7

natron, 29

Nephthys (god), 26

Nile River
  annual flooding, 23–25, **24**
  importance of, 22

use in construction of Great Pyramid, 35, 37, 49
  west bank, 35, 37

North Pyramid of Dahshur (Red Pyramid), 15, 19, 35

Opening of the Mouth ceremony, 23

Osiris (god), 26, 68

pharaoh, use of term, 8

plumb lines, 39, 40

priestesses, 66, 67, 68

pyramidion, 19, 49–50

Pyramid Rover (robot), 53

pyramids, **55**
  after Great Pyramid
    Djedefre's, 54–55
    Khafre's, 8, 55–57
    Menkaure's, 8, 42, 57–58
  boats in, 32, **51**, 52–53
  design perfected, 19–20
  as granaries, 10
  interior space of, 30, 46–47, **47**
  meaning of shape, 21
  as national building projects, 8
  number built, 15
  orientation of, 39–40, 62
  as part of larger complexes, 17
  proverb about time and, 71
  purpose of, 8, 32–33, 58
  small, 31–32
  See also specific structures

Pyramid Texts, 23, 25, 26

Queen's Chamber (Great Pyramid), 47, **47**, 49, 53

Queen's Pyramids, 32, **47**, 52

ramps, 41, 42–45, **43**, 56

Ra/Re (god)
  birth/death cycle and, 25–26
  creation and, 27
  feast of, 70
  importance of, 15, 20
  kings as son of, 54, 55

Red Pyramid, 15, 19, 35
Relieving Chambers, **47**, 48–49
religious beliefs
    about human spirit and body, 27–28
    building of pyramids and, 8, 10,
        32–33, 37
    curses and, 66
    cyclical events and, 25, 26
    east and west as symbols, 35
    flooding of Nile and, 25
    kings as gods, 8, 26–27
    number of deities, 27
    Pyramid Texts, 23, 25, 26
    See also afterlife; burial practices;
       specific gods
ren (name), 27
rockers, 44
roofs, corbelled, 16, 20

sacrifices, 12, 14, 23
sah (physical human body), 27
Saqqara mastabas, 11–12, **13**, 25
Second Dynasty burial practices, 11–12
Sed festival, 14
serdab (room in pyramid), 50
Seth (in creation myth), 68
Seven Wonders of the Ancient World, 7
shuwt (shadow), 27, 28
Smith, Craig B.
    on construction of Great Pyramid, 7,
        38–39, 49
    on Egyptians' beliefs, 10
    on Hemiunu at Khufu's funeral, 50
    on reason for mummification, 29–30
Sneferu (king)
    attempted pyramid conversion, 15
    Bent Pyramid, 15–19, 35
    Meidum pyramid, 15–16, **18**
    Red Pyramid, 15, 19
Sphinx, 41
square level, 39
Step Pyramid, 12–15, **13**, 19

storytelling, 63
stretching of the cord ceremony, 40
Sumerians, 25
sun
    god of
        birth/death cycle and, 25–26
        creation and, 27
        feast of, 70
        importance of, 15, 20
        kings as son of, 54, 55
    symbol of, 21–22

Third Dynasty burial practices, 12
tomb robbers
    curses against, 66
    frequency of, 31
    of Khafre's tomb, 57
    kings' attitudes about, 27
tombs. *See* mastabas
tourists, 7, 70
Twain, Mark, 7

visitors, 7, 70
Vyse, Howard, 57, 58

Watterson, Barbara, 66
Wepwawet (god), 14, 53
Wepwawet (robot), 53
Western Town, 68
Wet (embalmer), 26
White Nile River, 24
women
    burial of, 67–68
    Isis, 26, 68, 69
    legal rights of, 66
    marriage expectations for, 67
    mother and wives of Khufu, 52
    professions of, 65, 66, 67, 68
    rank of wives, 65
Wonders of the Ancient World, 7
work crews. *See* construction workers
wrappers, 26

PICTURE CREDITS

ABOUT THE AUTHORS

Charles and Linda George have written more than 70 nonfiction books for children and young adults—on topics as wide ranging as the Holocaust, world religions, the civil rights movement, ancient civilizations, climate change research, the Dalai Lama, and gene therapy. They retired from teaching in Texas public schools some years ago to write full-time. They live in a small town in west Texas.